Re-Reading the Postwar Period

Samir Amin

Re-Reading the Postwar Period: An Intellectual Itinerary

Translated by
Michael Wolfers

Monthly Review Press
New York

Library of Congress Cataloging-in-Publication Data

Amin, Samir.
[Itinéraire intellectuel. English]
   Re-reading the postwar period : an intellectual itinerary / by Samir Amin;
translated by Michael Wolfers.
      p.   cm.
   ISBN 0-85345-893-6 : $26.00 — ISBN 0-85345-894-4 (pbk.) : $14.00
   1. Economic history—1945– 2. World politics—1945– 3. Marxian economics.
4. Capitalism. I. Title.
HC59.A7852513 1994
330.9—dc20   94-14480
                                                  CIP

Monthly Review Press
122 West 27th Street
New York, NY 10001

Manufactured in the United States of America
10 9 8 7 6 5 4 3 2 1

Contents

5

Foreword

The purpose of this book is not to suggest a specific reading of the half century since World War II, but to provide some kind of intellectual autobiography. I am trying to retrace the steps I took in formulating my positions on capitalism and socialism. This requires placing my biography within the history of the period. I shall show successive moments of this history as I see them today and as I believe I felt them at the time. I have never kept a diary and I cannot be sure of avoiding a reinterpretation of the analyses and reactions I had at the time. The first chapter therefore gives a summary of the postwar period as I see it today.

Fortunately I can refer to dated and published writings on the positions whose history is examined in this book. The meaning of the ideas that are put forward is not absolute for author or reader, but conditional on the historic moment of their production. I shall try my utmost to explain this complex relationship between the reality of the living moment, the formulation of my analysis, and my expression of the latter.

My intellectual biography revolves around certain key issues that I have always tried to address. As early as my secondary school and university days, I supported the Marxist analysis of social reality and was convinced that socialism was the sole acceptable human response to the horrors of all kinds caused by capitalism.

One question stirred me intellectually more than any other: Why has the history of capitalist expansion been marked by polarization on a world scale? Why did the expansion not reduce the gap between the "developed" center and the "underdeveloped" periphery? I provide in this book a reading of my response to this key question, a response formulated as early as my doctoral thesis in 1957 but constantly reformulated and, I trust, progressively deepened.

Two comments: First, I have always sought to grasp capitalist polarization in its totality, to go beyond the narrow field of economic mechanisms and laws in which it is expressed and integrate the laws into an analysis based in historical materialism. Second, I have always demanded that my political conclusions suggest a direction for action.

The real question is whether the center-periphery polarization can gradually be wiped out under capitalism, allowing national bourgeois development to take place at the periphery. This question has constantly faced the movements for national liberation and socialism I have always supported. The varying, often ambiguous, responses to this question led to a variety of political approaches and positions. Of course, the question remains.

I shall show how my answer has evolved and has always remained essentially negative. In essence, I maintain that polarization is inherent in capitalism. Polarization is not the effect of concrete and specific circumstances in this or that case; rather, it is the effect of the law of accumulation on a world scale. From this general conclusion, I draw a number of political points.

The first point is whether the socialist alternative is a historical necessity. The Soviet model of socialism seems able to achieve precisely what capitalism cannot, namely a developmental "catching-up." It seems able to undo the historical effects of polarization through an accelerated development of the productive forces roughly comparable with those of advanced capitalism. But there is an essential contradiction facing those struggling for socialism. I summarize it as a choice between catching up and building an alternative society. Of course, this analysis is closely linked to my views on the true character of the genuine historical challenge presented by polarization.

The second point is that polarization has brought intolerable social conditions to the periphery, but the response by those affected has been, and seems likely to be, incomplete, ill-conceived, and disappointing. I base this on constant and direct participation in the national liberation movements of the third world. In this intellectual autobiography I shall try to retrace the steps I have taken to reach my current conclusions.

My intellectual concerns have never been narrowly academic. Rather, I have always thought of myself as a militant of socialism and of popular liberation. I have as far as possible put the wisdom I acquired through intellectual training to the service of the cause. I always felt responsible for the political approaches and options that flowed from my analyses. The analyses and their historical and political context are closely linked to the options for action. The guiding principle of my life has always been Karl Marx's thesis that "The philosophers have only *interpreted* the world in various ways; the point, however, is to *change* it."

I shall try in this book to retrace the close link between the shifts in my position and the evolution of world reality as I perceived it in all its economic, political, and cultural aspects. I shall indicate the historical landmarks that provide the essential signs of the reality at each step.

My stand also demands that I avoid a narrowly academic approach to writing. I have not hesitated to write a great deal. I regard writing as a significant social act. Unlike many academics, I do not try to produce a definitive work, but rather a piece of writing that is one step in an endless development process carried on by a collective of oneself and others. I do not aim to win over the academic world with a dazzling display of learning and references to the literature. I rely on my reasonable memory of sustained reading. When I write I always have in mind a more attractive public from my point of view, an audience of committed militant intellectuals.

I am and always have been an internationalist, and I am convinced that capitalism has created an objective situation that demands responses to concerted challenges operating on a world scale. People can respond effectively to the "capitalist international" only by shaping their own internationalism with a universalist scope transcending national cultural (and religious) horizons. However, I gaze on this universalist perspective from the periphery of the capitalist world, and particularly from the Afro-Asian world of non-European culture. I do so because it is the world to which I belong. I do so for the objective reason that this world is the main victim of actually existing capitalism. The social tragedies of all kinds that polarization has brought to people is the major challenge facing humankind. I have never been a "third worldist." I believe the term applies only to certain Western leftists who in the Bandung era (1955-1975) thought they could substitute "third world peoples" for the "proletariat" in expressing their messianic expectation. Although I felt genuine sympathy for them, I was conscious that their limitations arose from an inadequate analysis of the real nature of the challenge.

1

The Postwar Period, 1945-1992: An Overview

The past half-century can now be seen as the completion of a historic period. We are entering a new and probably markedly different cycle. With hindsight, the period just completed can be described more accurately than was possible even a few years ago.

The postwar system rested on three pillars: Fordism in the Western countries, Sovietism in the East European countries, and developmentalism in the third world. These pillars defined the social and political order for each of the regions and the economic, political, and ideological relations between them. The international order was itself the effect of confrontations between the dominant forces in each of the world's subsystems. These competing and complementary systems gradually wore down until at the end of the cycle they collapsed one after another.[1] A period of storms accompanied the restructuring and subsequent articulation along qualitatively new lines.

The postwar period may be subdivided into three phases.

ESTABLISHING THE GLOBAL ECONOMIC SYSTEM: 1945-1955

World War II provided the United States with an unexpected opportunity to escape from the deep crisis of the

1930s, to speed up the modernization of its productive system through diffusion of the Fordist model (begun in the 1920s), and to acquire a leadership role in all fields, sadly symbolized by the exercise of its nuclear monopoly in the August 1945 bombing of Hiroshima and Nagasaki. The backwardness of Europe and Japan (shown in the weak penetration of the Fordist model) was apparent in the wake of World War I and was aggravated by the exhausting struggles between victors and vanquished that followed the war. The backwardness reached dramatic proportions as a result of the massive destruction caused by World War II.

However, the European and Japanese social fabric was sufficiently strong to avoid a recurrence of the revolutionary radicalization of 1919. On the contrary, Europe under the Marshall Plan and Japan under the 1951 Treaty of San Francisco underwent speedy development on the Fordist model. The historic compromise between capital and labor that formed the basis of ideological regulation was still audible in 1919, although the ideological underpinning had been achieved through the massive recruitment of working classes by their imperialist bourgeoisies since the end of the nineteenth century and especially since 1914. Accordingly, what I call "Socialism I" was certainly over by then. In 1945 everything was set for speedy implementation of Fordism. Rapid modernization came within the framework of a U.S. hegemony that was accepted without reservation in the 1949 creation of NATO, despite some rhetorical rearguard actions fought by the old colonialists. The system was fully in place by the mid-1950s with the Japanese economic takeoff and the 1957 Treaty of Rome.

Sovietism crystallized in the 1930s. The Russian Revolution faced contradictory demands from the outset. Should priority be given to the need to catch up, meaning broadly replicating capitalist structures, or should the goal of building an alternative, classless society take precedence? From

1930 the first option was favored; the system gradually moved away from its original socialist aims.

Sovietism subsequently underwent a baptism of fire. It emerged victorious from its confrontation with Nazi rule and played a decisive part in defeating it. Despite massive losses in the war, the Soviet Union enjoyed enormous prestige in 1945 and was able to cross the first threshold of the Cold War declared on it by the United States. The USSR was on the defensive in 1945 and did not reach military parity with its American rival until the end of the 1960s. Hence I maintain that the bipolar international system was in place not under the Yalta Agreement, as is often too readily said, but after the Potsdam Conference. At Yalta the United States did not yet have nuclear weapons and was therefore obliged to accept the Soviet Union's demand for a protective flank in Eastern Europe against a possible recurrence of German militarism; at Potsdam, the United States, confident of military supremacy, decided to impose a debilitating arms race on the USSR.

Until Stalin's death in 1953, postwar Sovietism was on the defensive. In subsequent years it launched a counteroffensive by uniting with third world nationalism and supporting the Bandung front established in 1955. For complex reasons related to differences between Maoism and Sovietism and a divergent view of third world revolt, a split between the two great powers of the Eastern world occurred after 1957.

At the end of World War II the African and Asian countries on the periphery of the world capitalist system were still subject to colonial rule. From 1800 on, the center-periphery polarization took the form of a contrast between industrialized areas and areas linked to colonialism and deprived of industry. The peoples of Asia and Africa, inspired by half a century of ideological and political redefinition around a new nationalism, burst into revolt after 1945. In the ensuing fifteen years, first Asia, then Africa regained their political independence. Everything was set for what Bandung called new "developmentalism": independence, modernization, industrialization. The strategic alliance between this movement and the Soviet Union enabled the latter to escape isolation.

A dialogue was opened between the Afro-Asian movement and that in Latin America, which was not faced with the struggle for political independence and the affirmation of a non-European culture but was concerned with the demands of modernization and industrialization of the continent.

THE BANDUNG ERA: 1955–1975

If I define Bandung as the dominant characteristic of the second phase of the postwar period, it is not from any "third worldist" predilection, but because the world system was organized around the emergence of the third world.

Modernization and industrialization brought radical change to Asia, Africa, and Latin America, in varying degrees that will be discussed in detail in this book. The world of today and tomorrow can no longer be what it was in the five previous centuries of capitalist deployment. Accumulation of capital on a world scale has taken on a new dimension.

The Bandung era, with the triumph of the ideology of development, was based on a range of seeming truths, specific to each region of the world but all deeply rooted in prevailing beliefs: Keynesianism; the myth of catching up through Soviet-style "socialism"; and the myth of catching up through third world interdependence. These prevailing myths have been subject to critical examination, but to a limited and little-understood degree.

Throughout the period the third world was the stage for constant confrontation between various "developmentalist" lines of differing degrees of social, ideological, and cultural radicalism. Maoism between 1965 and 1975 represents the apogee. During this period the Soviet Union escaped from its isolation by allying with the rising tide of third world national liberation. This gave the world system the appearance of a bipolarity determined by conflict between two superpowers. It was only a matter of appearances. The Soviet Union gradually wore itself down in the arms race imposed by Washington. The strategic goal of the Soviet Union's efforts to smash NATO was not to conquer Europe or to export "socialism," but merely to end U.S. world hegemony and replace it with peaceful coexistence in a multicentric world. The strategy has finally failed.

Throughout the period, Western capital has remained glued to the United States, not through fear of Soviet expansionism—the Western ruling class knew this was an unreal danger despite manipulation of public opinion—but for the profound reason that capitalist accumulation was penetrating on a world scale. Europe and Japan made advances but did not perceive their conflict with the United States as analogous to imperialist conflicts in previous stages of history.

THE COLLAPSE OF THE GLOBAL SYSTEM: 1975-1992

The third phase of the postwar cycle saw the collapse of the three pillars on which internal and world order rested. The crisis began in the capitalist West and called into question the myth of unlimited growth, with 1968 as the decisive turning point. The subsequent years offered hope for a possible revival of a Western left stupefied by a pro-imperialist recruitment from the end of the nineteenth century. Such hopes were rapidly extinguished in inconsistent projects. By 1980 the way was open for a neoliberal offensive that held sway but could not lead the Western societies out of the dark tunnel of prolonged crisis or revive the illusions of unlimited growth.

In turn a hardening of North-South relations accompanying the crisis of capitalist accumulation hastened the disillusionment with developmentalism in the third world. Radical regimes collapsed one after the other and surrendered to reactionary structural adjustment policies imposed by the West during the 1980s. The collapse was the result not of external aggression but of a combination of the internal contradictions of the Bandung project and a new external crisis accompanying the overthrow of the existing world system.

The failure of the Bandung project also revealed the weakness of Soviet support. Sovietism, the third pillar of the postwar system, had the most shattering collapse. The edifice seemed so solid that conservative ideologues described it as "irreversible totalitarianism." But it was gnawed away from within and collapsed in the space of a few months, leaving behind nothing but chaos. Here too, of course, collapse resulted from a dramatic acceleration in the Soviet Union's "conventional" capitalism, as well as from external factors, namely, Washington's victory in the arms race.

History never stops. The completed postwar cycle can also be seen as a transition between what came before and what follows. At the end of World War II, actually existing capitalism still retained certain fundamental characteristics of its historical heritage.

The historically constructed national bourgeois states formed the political and social framework for national capitalist economies, with national productive systems broadly controlled and directed by national capital; these states were in strong competition with each other and together constituted the centers of the world system. After the centers had their successive industrial revolutions during the nineteenth century, there was a near total distinction between industrialization at the center and absence of industry at the periphery.

Since World War II both characteristics have gradually changed. After regaining their political independence, the peripheries embarked on industrialization, although on unequal terms, to the point that apparent homogeneity previously induced by a shared lack of industry gave way to increasing differentiation between a semi-industrialized third world and a fourth world that had not begun to industrialize. Capitalist globalization throughout the centers broke through the boundaries of national productive systems and began to reshape them as segments of a worldwide productive system.

The postwar cycle may now be regarded as a period of transition between the old system and the new. The essential characteristics of the new system need to be described, and its contradictions and trends identified. The uneven development at the periphery and the globalization of capital are the main challenges facing theoretical analysis and social and political practice.

Is third world industrialization the start of a geographical spread of capitalism that will gradually obliterate the center-periphery polarization? Or will the polarization be replicated in new forms? If so, what forms?

Is the lack of industrialization in the "fourth world" a mere delay in the homogenizing expansion of capitalism on a world scale? Is the delay attributable to internal factors specific to the societies in question or to profound laws whereby polarization differentiates among the peripheral countries and marginalizes some of them? Does the decline of efficiency in the nation-states require an alternative system of political management of the capitalist system on national and world scales? Are we on the road to building such a system? If so, what will its characteristics be and what laws will operate?

To answer these questions we must take into account both the laws governing capital accumulation and the political and ideological responses of different social sectors to the expansion of capitalism. The future remains uncertain. Actually existing capitalism must adapt to the political solutions of the struggles occasioned by the conflict of social interests.

I shall summarize the answer I have given in recent years. Third world industrialization will not end the polarization that I believe is inherent in world capitalism. It will shift the mechanisms and forms to other levels determined by the financial, technological, cultural, and military monopolies enjoyed by the centers, but it will not replicate the developed countries' social evolution. Western society was first transformed by the Industrial Revolution and the ongoing agricultural revolution. The vast lands of the Americas served as an escape valve for the pressure brought by European population growth, while colonial conquest assured an abundance of cheap raw materials. Fordism came along to alleviate the historic tension between capital and labor, facilitated by the reduction of the reserve army of labor in the centers. By contrast, the industrializing third world has none of these favorable factors to soften the savage effects of expanding capitalism. Here the coexistence of a rapidly increasing active labor army and an ever plentiful reserve labor army leads to acute and potentially revolutionary social conflict. This characteristic situation of modern peripheral capitalism creates political and ideological circumstances conducive to the formation of popular alliances between the active working class, the peasants, and the impoverished marginalized masses in the reserve army of labor.

In the fourth world the social system becomes grotesque. The overwhelming majority are the marginalized poor and peasant masses excluded from any agricultural revolution. The minority ruling class can make no claim to historical legitimacy. Struggles in the workplace are weak because of the marginalization, so the conflict shifts to the cultural plane. This is symptomatic of the crisis but offers no genuine response to its challenge.

In the developed West the conflict between the globalization of capital penetration eroding the historic role of the nation-state as the management framework for historic social compromises and the permanence of political and ideological systems based on national realities will not be easily resolved. Neither U.S. military hegemony nor a German-dominated European "supermarket" can resolve the problem. Dividing responsibilities on a regional basis by linking various parts of the South and the East to one of the three centers in the developed North or West is no answer, either. In the short term the Soviet collapse is bound to bring a capitalist expansion similar to that of the periphery. Social democratic responses along Western models will not be allowed to develop here.

During the postwar cycle political and ideological conflicts and the expression of progressive alternative projects have been constrained by the historical shortcomings of the three prevailing ideologies: Western social democracy, Eastern Sovietism, and Southern national liberation ideology. The left on a world scale has shown signs in the recent past of going beyond these visions.

The unexpected crisis in Europe in the mid-1970s gave hopes of a leftist revival and a redefinition of the socialist outlook free of the dogma of the old social democracy, whose success was closely linked to postwar modernization and the dogma of Sovietism. These hopes were speedily dashed, and the retreat of social democracy has so far redounded to the benefit of the old right.

In third world countries there was constant debate and often violent conflict between moderates favoring state power in the Bandung mold and others who argued that radicalization was the only possible response to the decline of non-democratic populism and its inevitable cooptation by world capitalism. These debates form a background to the discussion in this book.

The debate revolved around a central issue: What is actually existing capitalism? Had it achieved its historic role? What was the struggle for socialism? This debate led naturally to questioning Sovietism. From the mid-1950s— and more precisely after the Twentieth Congress of the Communist Party of the Soviet Union in 1956—Stalinism became subject to criticism. While the prevailing critique made in the Soviet Union—from Khrushchev to Gorbachev—came from the right, in the 1960s and 1970s Maoism offered a critique from the left.

These issues must be picked up again today. The rapid collapse of the myths of the postwar period enables us to go much further than before. World War I ended the first cycle of the development of socialist thought and action. The second cycle, initiated by the Russian Revolution, is also closed. In response to the challenge of capitalism, which has itself embarked on a new cycle of operations, the third cycle of socialism remains to be built.

If a new socialist alternative is not developed, and if progressive social and ideological forces do not struggle for that alternative, the contradictions within capitalism will not generate a "new order" (as the neoliberals in power everywhere like to call it), but merely catastrophic chaos.

2

Establishing the Global Economic System, 1945-1955

The war years and the ensuing decade corresponded with my adolescence and university studies. I shall in this chapter refer to the landmarks of my personal life to locate myself in the period.

I was born in Cairo in 1931 to an Egyptian father and French mother, both doctors. I spent my childhood and adolescence in Port Said and attended the town's French *lycée*. I received my high school diploma in 1947 and left for Paris to attend university.

I have a very clear memory of the war years when I was at high school, and an equally clear memory of the reasons why I came to support the ideal of socialism as early as adolescence. My primary reason was foremost a revulsion against the wretchedness to which local children of my own age were condemned. Although the majority of young people from the privileged social class to which I belonged seemed to accept the state of things as almost natural, I decided to join the movement for social revolution that is essential to changing the world. I owe this choice largely to my family upbringing, which taught me that surrender to an unjust order is not acceptable. I then came to the conclusion that we must act "like the Russians," who had resolved the issue by building a new and ideal society where all these problems had been solved. From about 1942 (I recall how I followed the battle of Stalingrad with anguish, then delight at the outcome), I pronounced myself a "communist," although at the age of eleven I was not sure what that meant. I did know the essential: that society must ensure genuine equality for all human beings in all countries of the world. I have never renounced that ideal; it is the only touchstone that keeps political and social action from sliding into opportunism.

At school I was more passionate about history than any other subject. Through history, I was going to acquire the intellectual equipment necessary to understand the world, its evolution, and the way to change it. In the French schools of the period, history was generally taught in an open and progressive manner. This broadly reflected the position of French culture in Egypt. My country was occupied by the British, and although formally independent since 1922, it was still under the foreign yoke. France, although an imperialist power like Britain, had been ousted from Egypt by its British rival. The schools of the lay cultural mission did not share the goal of the Egyptian state schools—or worse, the English-language schools—of training officials for the existing system; rather, they regarded the system with a cautiously critical eye. Egypt's long and glorious history and the French Revolution were both stressed. We were encouraged to claim our independence—natural in a country such as ours—and to adopt progressive attitudes. Gradually I saw the connection between the wretched social situation of the Egyptian people and the country's submission to imperialist domination. I soon defined myself not only as a communist but also as an anti-imperialist.

I chose my reading accordingly. After reading Jules Verne, I plunged with delight into Zola, whose denunciation of the conditions of the working class inspired me, then a little later into Balzac, whose portrayal of bourgeois society and its cynicism excited me just as much. From the age of fourteen I was irresistibly drawn to Marxist texts. Cairo had a library that allowed access to this literature. So alongside my desire to understand history I read *The*

Eighteenth Brumaire of Louis Bonaparte, The Civil War in France, State and Revolution, Imperialism, the Highest Stage of Capitalism, etc. Then a year later I made up my mind to read *Capital* and did so into the next year, not that I gathered much from the first reading.

At high school most of the young Egyptians of my age were also anti-imperialist and therefore drawn to Marxism. Many of these young people became Egyptian Communist activists despite their privileged class origin. For many of them awareness of the social problem followed that of the national problem, whereas my trajectory was the reverse.

I arrived in Paris in 1947 to enroll at the Lycée Henri IV in higher mathematics. It is axiomatic that I immediately joined the Communist Party and became active in the school cell. Regarding higher studies I hesitated between physics and mathematics and social sciences. In the end I opted for the latter simply because these studies gave an opening to a professional life closer to my concerns for militant action. It was a choice that was sorely felt by my physical science teachers and my parents. I decided to study law (in France at the time one could only study economics through the law faculty) and enrolled in the Institute of Political Studies. I received my political science diploma in 1952 and my economic law degree in 1953. I decided to study for a doctorate in economics and enrolled at the University of Paris Institute of Statistics, to make use of my mathematical skills. In 1956 I received a diploma in statistics. I presented my state doctoral thesis in economics in June 1957 and returned to Egypt in August of that year.

During my ten years in Paris I spent most of my time in militant action and only the minimum on university work. I opted for militant action in the overseas student movement, where Egyptians were shoulder to shoulder with other Arabs and Africans, Vietnamese and other Asians. The active Communist groups of these nationalities often played a leadership role in the anti-imperialist mass associations. The initiative we displayed and the openness of this broad front clashed with the dogmatic spirit and defensive closeness in which Western Communism of the time was obliged to operate. Our journal, *Étudiants Anticolonialistes* (1949-1953), was not always looked on with favor at Number 44, the headquarters of the Central Committee of the French Communist Party (PCF).[1] Although accused of all kinds of nationalist or petty bourgeois "deviations," we doggedly followed our own line. This later encouraged us to move rapidly toward Maoism and to an understanding of why and how Soviet "revisionism" had embarked on the path to restoring capitalism. Subsequent events confirmed these precocious leanings.

Militant action brought me into close touch with many people who would later hold leading positions—as neocolonialists, populists, or revolutionaries—in independent Africa.[2] It was in the Communist cell at the Institute of Political Studies that I met Isabelle, with whom I have lived ever since.

The French university of the time was different from what it became later. With certain exceptions, such as the Marxist lectures by Jean Baby at the Institute of Political Studies, we did not usually go to lectures. Instead, we read widely and deeply. A student such as I, who had a genuine interest in social and economic thought, would read all the classics: Marx, of course—including *Capital*—plus Ricardo, Smith, Böhm-Bawerk, Walras, Keynes, and so on. It was unthinkable to "learn" economics through lectures and in textbooks such as Paul Samuelson's, as has become the rule in succeeding generations. I believe that this much more serious training made us absorb in depth the Marxist critique of bourgeois thought and to take account of the internal critique of the prevailing economistic thinking. We discovered its tendency to legitimize capitalism through an ahistorical formulation of the mechanisms to assure the rule of "universal harmonies."

For my part I found that the actually existing capitalist world was anything but harmonious: the underdevelopment in which three-quarters of humankind was trapped must be explained by the laws of capitalism; the reality of imperialism went against the artificial separation of politics and economics. Historical materialism provided the only scientific method worthy of the name.

I decided to consider this matter of "underdevelopment" in a doctoral thesis. The emergence of Asian and African nations through the victory of the national liberation movement was one of the era's main characteristics. The national liberation movement and the establishment of a dominant world system raised the development issue. A new literature, gradually crystallizing into one or several theories of development, or even an ideology of development, made its first appearance after 1950.

When I began my doctoral preparation, the literature from those the World Bank forty years later called "pioneers in development" was still meager. A student such as I could set out to read the whole of this literature. This is what I did, with the aim of offering a precocious critique of these "pioneers," trapped in conventional logic and patterns of bourgeois economics and sociology. Nowadays there are so many economics publications that an exhaustive reading of the literature on the subject is quite out of the question. This increase has not advanced understanding of the world, although it has allowed an accumulation of case studies. Nowadays economic literature is repetitive and is bogged down in detail and the artificial game of modelling.

With hindsight we can see that the first postwar decade was the period of the establishment of the system that would operate in the 1960s and reach crisis in the 1970s and 1980s. The United States emerged from the war with a revived and flourishing economy—the only one of the time—with a monopoly on the ultimate weapon. It decided at the Potsdam Conference in 1945 to attack the USSR and to establish world hegemony by imposing a Cold War. This was dreamed up by Churchill, who had not forgotten the defeat of the imperialist powers when they tried to over-throw the Russian Revolution after World War I. As a first step, the United States had to recruit Western Europe and achieve a reconciliation with the vanquished—Germany and Japan. The American people were ideologically prepared for this policy by an unprecedented hammering of Communism that culminated in semi-fascist state-sponsored McCarthyism and the odious Rosenberg trial.

U.S. strategy in Europe and Japan soon achieved total success, thanks to the unconditional recruitment of the entire bourgeoisie and all political parties, including socialist and social democratic parties. Communist parties were isolated after their exclusion from government in France and Italy in 1947. The Marshall Plan paved the way for a rapid rebuilding of Europe, where the United States encouraged reconciliation and a commitment to economic integration. The Organization for European Economic Cooperation was created, which became the Organization for Economic Cooperation and Development (OECD) in 1961; it was followed by the Council of Europe in 1949, the European Coal and Steel Community (ECSC) in 1951, and the Treaty of Rome in 1957. These bodies were not conceived to build a Europe able to compete with the United States and achieve autonomy, but to create a subsystem of an open worldwide system necessary for U.S. hegemony. The groundwork for the Fordist expansion of the 1960s was laid at the economic level (gradual globalization of the market), and at the social and political level (the historic compromise between capital and labor). In Japan, the San Francisco Treaty of 1951, the establishment of a controlled democracy, and the reconstitution of the *zaibatsu* oligopolies were preliminary to the takeoff of following years.

From the start the strategy of U.S. hegemony was to establish an anti-Soviet military bloc with the United States in the political leadership role. The Truman doctrine (1947); the creation of NATO (1949); the admission into NATO of Turkey, Greece, and Germany (1952); the incorporation of Portugal (1951) and Spain (1953) into the U.S. military system, although these two countries remained fascist; and the San Francisco Treaty (1951), complemented later by the U.S.-Japan security pact (1960), were part of this dimension of military control within the U.S. hegemonic strategy.

In the face of this deployment, the USSR remained in isolation and on the defensive until the mid-1950s. It was obliged to join the arms race to end the U.S. monopoly in this field. At Yalta the USSR gained the right to establish a protective flank in Eastern Europe, but no more. The establishment of supporting regimes in the region created difficulties that were never really overcome. The anticapitalist and antifascist social forces were too weak to take power alone (Poland, Hungary, Rumania). Or the local Communists did take power by liberating their countries from the Fascist yoke (Yugoslavia and Albania) and had no intention of becoming agents of Soviet policy. However, we accepted the establishment of these regimes. What was the alternative? The terrible repression of Greek Communism (1945-1948) showed us that the West would not have established anything other than fascist regimes in Eastern Europe. Even the pro-Western populism of Kemal Atatürk's Turkey did not seem to suit them, and so imperialism imposed Menderes in 1950 through multiparty elections. The strategy was repeated later in many third world countries.

The creation of the Cominform in 1947 had the goal of legitimizing the defensive posture of the USSR by closing ranks around the Communist Party of the Soviet Union. The Zhdanov doctrine (1948) divided the world into two camps—capitalist and socialist—assigned the countries of the West and the East to each of the camps, and overlooked the third world liberation movement.

Moscow met difficulties in its strategy of consolidating its protective flank, as indicated by the series of trials against opponents from the right and left in the new people's democracies (1947-1948), the condemnation of Titoism (1948), the attempted blockade of Berlin (1948-1949), and signs of revolt in Yugoslavia and Berlin (1951). The Council for Mutual Economic Assistance (Comecon) was created in 1949 in response to the Marshall Plan, but it never really coordinated the development plans of countries in the region. The Warsaw Pact was formed in 1955 in response to NATO.

After the death of Stalin in 1953 and the Twentieth Congress of the CPSU in 1956, the USSR embarked on a new strategy aimed at breaking the previous isolation through an alliance with the third world, whose emergence was signaled in the Bandung conference of 1955. The Soviet system began to catch up militarily (Sputnik was launched in 1957) but remained politically weak, as the uprisings in Poznan and Budapest showed.

The real obstacle to U.S. hegemony came from the Afro-Asian national liberation movement. The countries in these regions were determined to throw off the colonial yoke of the nineteenth century. Imperialism has never been able to make the social and political compromises necessary to install stable powers operating to its advantage in the countries of the capitalist periphery. I interpret this failure, about which I shall have more to say, as evidence that such compromise is objectively unattainable, that the polarization caused by capitalist expansion creates in the periphery an objective situation that is by its very nature explosive and unstable, and potentially revolutionary.

Fifteen years after World War II the world political structure had been radically transformed. For the first time in history the system of sovereign states was extended to the entire globe. From the time of the Treaty of Westphalia in 1648, when this system replaced Christian feudalism, through the Congress of Vienna in 1815 to the Treaty of Versailles in 1919, this system had been restricted to the West. The United States was integrated in a second phase from the proclamation of the Monroe Doctrine in 1823 to the formation of the League of Nations in 1922. Asia and Africa were treated as nonsovereign spaces—fair game for competitive expansion from the centers. The formation of the United Nations in 1945, and particularly the winning of independence by the peoples of Asia and Africa from 1945 to 1960, brought a qualitative change in the political organization of the world capitalist system.

The transformation came about through the national liberation struggles that mobilized all the peoples of Asia and Africa. Imperialism never made the slightest concession without a struggle. The formation of our current international system is not something that capitalism sought and planned for. On the contrary, it is the result of global capital's successful short-term adjustment to changes forced on it. The hegemonic power of the postwar system—the United States—adapted more readily than the old colonial powers in decline, and in the case of the weakest national liberation movements surrendering to neocolonial compromise, it could sometimes even appear to support the evolution. Conversely, the United States led the imperialist fight against the strongest radical movements—those that were led by Communist parties (China, Vietnam, Cuba) or by determined nationalists supported by a radicalized popular movement (Nasserism, Arab and African socialism). The United States was our principal enemy. Naturally, Europe and Japan were in solidarity with the hegemonic power.

Of course the qualitative transformation in the world political system considered here is not the "end of history," nor does it guarantee any real stability. The new hierarchy of powers appearing after 1980 only provides a semblance of stability. There is no firm historical compromise that will bring stability.

There is no doubt that the great tide of national liberation (1945-1975) was marked by real gains for Asia, Africa, and Latin America. But the advances were inadequate since they fell short of their goal. By the end of the postwar cycle, third world states were turned back into a comprador role. It is of little interest to make a global assessment of the pluses and minuses. The ever present question was where and how far the movement could go to create the most favorable conditions for long-term change.

The most striking advances were made in China, then Vietnam and Korea, where the fight for national liberation was merged with the fight for socialism. From 1947 to 1949 I followed the progress of the People's Liberation Army on the map of China. I read Mao Zedong's *On New Democracy* (1940) in a French edition and accepted the view that the age was no longer one of bourgeois revolution because the colonial bourgeoisie had joined the imperialist project for expansion. Rather, it was the period of socialist revolution, developing in an unbroken succession on the periphery of the capitalist system. The democratic, anti-imperialist revolution was led by the proletariat and its (Communist) party in close alliance with the peasantry. It neutralized the national bourgeoisie and isolated the comprador feudal bloc. The circumstances were ripe for speedy passage to the building of socialism.

I saw that North Korea was engaged in a similar process. The local anti-imperialist front had liberated the country from Japanese colonialists, although it was later obliged by the military context of Japanese capitulation to surrender the southern part of the country to the dictatorship established by the U.S. occupying forces. I saw that Vietnam was also following this path after 1945. The appalling colonial war waged by France with U.S. support until their defeat at Dien Bien Phu in 1954 attested to imperialism's determination to keep national liberation off the agenda. The Geneva agreement in 1954 and the provisional partition of the country seemed to me justified, as I believed that in a second phase struggle in the south would achieve its goal. The Korean war (1950-1953) was further evidence of the collective will of the imperialists to oppose the movement. The refusal to recognize the People's Republic of China and the isolation imposed by the West were reminiscent of earlier imperialist attitudes toward the Russian Revolution.

The success of the national liberation movement was reckoned by its greatest advances. I believed that any liberation that did not go this far had not completed its task. I believed the objective conditions existed to complete the task throughout Asia and Africa, beginning with Egypt.

Like all young Egyptians of the time I was excited by the radicalization of the anti-imperialist and popular social movement, which culminated in the general strike of February 21, 1946, and by the success of the new Communist movement. The first Communist party, founded in the wake of the Russian Revolution, had been subject to severe repression and was virtually wiped out in the 1930s. Revived in World War II, it quickly won the respect of all those in Egypt with a patriotic and social conscience. It was the sole force opposing the monarchy that was loathed by politicized elements of the popular classes and the radicalized petty bourgeoisie. It seemed capable of leading a united front similar to those in China and Vietnam. Egypt had never enjoyed any genuine democracy in its modern history and repression was a constant. The exploiting classes and the imperialist powers feared Communism. This did not prevent the red flag from waving over the Nile Valley. A genuine bourgeois democracy at the time would have allowed the Communists to win mass support, and possibly even elections. Neither the bourgeoisie nor the Western powers could run that risk.

The establishment of the state of Israel and the first Palestine war in 1948 gave the local reactionary forces breathing space. The debate around the 1948 events ensured the collapse of the monarchy, the central political pillar of imperialist and reactionary domination. The Wafdist electoral victory in 1950, the demand to abrogate the unjust Anglo-Egyptian treaty of 1936, and the beginning of partisan action against the occupied Suez Canal zone gave hope that an antifeudal, anticomprador revolution was feasible. The burning of Cairo (early 1952), the ousting of the Wafdist government, and the ensuing ungovernability of the country led to the Free Officers' Coup in July 1952. This simultaneously raised hopes of possible social advance and cut the ground out from under the feet of the progressive forces.

Nasserism nurtured hopes of Western support. Egypt made all the necessary concessions, but ultimately it came to realize that it could expect nothing from the United States. After the tripartite declaration of 1950 (United States, Great Britain, and France), the United States sought to control the entire region through compliant regimes in Israel and Turkey. The United States required the Arabs to join military pacts (on the pretext of a nonexistent Soviet threat) and took over from the discomfited British and French protectorates. When Nasser refused to sign the Baghdad pact in 1954, Washington began an offensive to overthrow him. This was the precise moment of the crystallization of the Bandung front. The USSR arranged for a delivery of Czech weapons to Egypt. In response to Egypt's support for the Algerian Front de Libération Nationale (FLN) and the nationalization of the Suez Canal, France and Britain set out to bring Nasser down. The conservatives in London and the socialists in Paris were shoulder to shoulder, but they failed in this final colonial adventure because they had forgotten they could act only according to U.S. plans and instructions. This opened a new chapter for national liberation in Egypt under circumstances very different from those of the previous decade. The bourgeoisie in Egypt, and elsewhere, resumed or seemed to resume leadership of national liberation, in contradiction with the fundamental positions I had supported since 1945.

The Mashreq (West Asia) prepared to challenge the uneasy balances of the period between the world wars. The establishment of the Ba'ath Party, which would determine the fate of the region from the end of the 1950s on, did not go unnoticed, any more than the ideological competition between the Communist and Ba'ath movements. We were skeptical about the Ba'ath Party's anti-imperialist stance and disturbed by its sometimes fascist style. After the riots at Setif in 1945 and in Tunisia in 1952, we knew that the days of colonial power in the Maghreb (northwest Africa) were numbered. But who would lead the liberation? Could neocolonial order be imposed by the Moroccan monarchy and the Tunisian bourgeoisie to whom France handed power in 1956? Would the powerful grassroots movement of the Algerian FLN overcome the anticommunism of its leaders? The anticommunism was fueled, all too sadly, by the servile attitude of the Maghreb Communists to the French Communist Party (PCF), whose policy was at best ambiguous.

The apparent power of the Tudeh Party in Iran fueled our optimism, despite the Soviet abandonment of the autonomous republics of Azerbaijan and Kurdistan in 1945. The chauvinism the Shah exploited through this was short-lived. Mossadegh nationalized oil during his brief period in power (1951-1953), but with his overthrow, the Shah's bloody dictatorship was ensured for a quarter of a century. In 1954, Iran and Turkey aligned with the United States, which was subjecting the entire region to its mania for pacts.

Because of the solidarity between our group of young Egyptians and black African students, I followed the

embryonic sub-Saharan liberation struggles with great enthusiasm. The Rassemblement Democratique Africain
(RDA) had just held its founding congress at Bamako,
signalling the certain end of colonialism. In 1951 came the
distressing "treachery" of the RDA's break with the PCF
(although the latter's policy of supporting the French
Union also seemed to us ambiguous). Were there any social
and political forces with more vision than these moderates,
to whom the colonial powers would later entrust the task
of managing neocolonialism? The ruthlessly quelled rebellion in Madagascar in 1947, the Mau Mau rebellion in Kenya
in 1952, and the guerrilla action waged by the Union des
Populations Camerounaises in Cameroon in 1955 all suggested that such forces existed. We were delighted by the
foundation of the Parti Africain de l'Indépendance (PAI)
in Senegal in 1957. We did not think that imperialism was
over and that Western "democracies" had suddenly taken
note of the intolerable injustice of colonialism when Ghana
gained independence in 1957, when the All-African Peoples
Conference met in Accra in 1958, when at last the French
government envisaged autonomy for its colonies in a
French community. We believed that the African peoples
had forced the change and that imperialism was merely
trying to preempt radicalization of their liberation struggle.

   We were convinced that the Asian and African liberation
struggles were in the foreground of the world scene after
1945. We also believed that we must count on our own
resources, as the USSR and China in defensive isolation
could offer only moral support. We did not expect much
from the prevailing Western orthodoxy. The socialists and
social democrats were renowned in all the colonial wars.
Even the PCF, on its own and taking a brave stand over
the Vietnam war, gradually succumbed to chauvinist pressures over Algeria and Africa. The Fourth Republic was
brought down by a dogged Algerian people's struggle and
the equivocation of French democrats in the face of fascist

agitation from the settlers. Would the new Gaullist regime take a tougher line on the Algerian war? We feared so—but we were wrong.

We judged national liberation by the standard of the victories in China and Vietnam. We attributed the same potential to the liberation and partisan wars throughout Southeast Asia after 1945—in Indonesia, the Philippines, Malaysia, and Thailand. In the early 1950s, the reactionary powers or local moderate nationalists took over and established a measure of internal order. We believed this was only a temporary setback. We thought that in the new Bandung era the conflict between imperialism and third world nations would take a different shape from before.

We also believed that the partition of India in 1947 and the establishment of Congress Party rule were major victories for imperialism. Imperialism had been able to call a brutal halt to a Chinese-style liberation war. The diplomatic rapprochement between Nehru's India and China and the signing of a treaty over Tibet in 1954 seemed to us positive, but our opinion of the Congress Party did not change. The year after Bandung things began to look different.

When I was at university, Latin America seemed a distant unknown. We had a better understanding of what was happening in the Caribbean—in Haiti, Jamaica, or Guadeloupe—than of the politics of Brazil, Mexico, or Argentina. I found out about the problems of Latin America when I read the first reports of the UN Economic Commission for Latin America under its mentor Raul Prebisch.

We had no awareness of the purpose and effect of Latin American populism of the 1930s and 1940s and saw it through the eyes of the Brazilian, Argentine, and Mexican Communist parties. If we saw populism as too moderate for the challenge, the United States still saw it as an adversary to be conquered. Vargas was deposed by the Brazilian military in 1945. Batista seized power in Cuba in 1952. Peron was overthrown in Argentina in 1955.

These events showed that the United States could and would dominate the continent only through loathsome and obedient dictatorships, corralled together in 1948 in the Organization of American States. The OAS complemented the inter-American defense agreement signed at Rio de Janeiro in 1947—a new expression of the Monroe Doctrine. We were therefore only too ready to support the new liberation movement launched by Fidel Castro.

I have attempted here to portray the events of the first postwar decade as I experienced them at the time. I retain today the same overall perception of this evolution, although I obviously could not foresee that it would lead to the new Bandung phase of liberation and progress for our societies in Asia and Africa. As of that date the conflict was to be waged in very different circumstances.

Until the late 1950s and the Sino-Soviet split in 1956, I shared the prevailing Marxist-Leninist view of the basic nature of socialism and socialist construction in the USSR. I had not yet realized that the theory of capitalist polarization which I had begun to formulate in my doctoral thesis called for a rethinking of the challenge posed by actually existing capitalism. On the other hand, some of us were not fooled by the idyllic image of a perfect society furnished by Soviet propaganda. We had traveled in "socialist" countries, noted the absence of democracy, and read enough to be aware of brutal repression. But two other factors that Western Communists tended to overlook seemed to us more significant than the shortcomings of Sovietism.

The first was the intransigent hostility of the Western powers to the Soviet Union (I am thinking of McCarthyism, or thirty years later the Reagan and Bush image of the "Evil Empire"). We knew that the Soviet Union was on the defensive, but the level of the West's hostility led us to believe that the country's system represented a real threat to capitalism. We never thought for a moment that any sane Western politician could believe that Stalin had any intention of invading Western Europe. Our solidarity with the USSR did not require total belief in the system. We had become used to the thought that since 1492 the Western powers had never intervened in any third world area for any justifiable cause, but always and without exception to harm the people. We believed almost spontaneously that imperialist capitalism could not allow any country to refuse its dictates. The West blamed the USSR for doing just that.

The second factor was that we had a much more radical critique of bourgeois democracy than did many Western progressives. We saw every day how such democracy was systematically denied our peoples and how Western diplomacy only sought democracy when it was in its tactical interests to do so. There has been no change in this. The argument for bourgeois "democracy" has no psychological appeal. Socialism or any popular advance must be more democratic than any bourgeois democracy. We turned their argument on its head. However, when it came to our own countries we were justifiably strict about the democratic shortfall of the populist nationalist regimes. Our doubts and criticisms of Nasserism from the outset were on this score. We were right, but we should have seen that this argument also applied to the USSR.

About the general crisis of capitalism, as portrayed in the Soviet terminology of the time, we were highly optimistic. We believed that the objective conditions were essentially the same as China's for all or nearly all third world countries. Hence radical national liberation struggles and the quest for socialist revolution were on the agenda. The later emergence from Bandung of a new national bourgeois initiative shows in retrospect that we oversimplified. We did not believe that socialist revolution was on the agenda except on the periphery of the system. This brought much soul-searching, especially in the relations between our overseas student movement (and our journal

Étudiants Anticolonialistes) and a French Communist Party that sacrificed colonial independence on the altar of an illusory socialist reconstruction of France, which would sweep dependent territories into the revolution.

Of course I was particularly conscious of the struggles waged in Egypt and the Arab world between 1945 and 1957. The journal *Moyen Orient*, published in Paris from 1949 to 1953, was a faithful but partial mirror of our concerns of the time, as the emphasis in the magazine was on the international aspects of the conflicts.[3] With hindsight, the analysis of the time seems to have hit the nail on the head.

The Palestine issue was always a major concern for us. In December 1947, the USSR supported the partition of Palestine, as did all the Communist parties of the time, including those in the Arab world. This provoked spirited debate and conflict, followed by well-meant self-criticism which was, in my view, insufficiently grounded. The Third International and the Egyptian and Arab Communists have always condemned Zionism, not only as nationalist and racist but also because it promotes a settlement colony that denies indigenous Palestinians the right to existence. The Egyptian Communist movement may still be proud of supporting the anti-Zionist trend among progressive Jews in Egypt since the 1940s. It has no need of self-criticism on this point even if Zionist propaganda has been quick to confuse anti-Zionism and anti-Semitism.

The partition of Palestine deserves closer examination. What tends to be forgotten is that the Soviet Union and the Arab, Palestinian, and Egyptian democratic forces sought independence for a unified, secular Palestinian state open to all its inhabitants, including recent Jewish immigrants. This last was no mean concession. Zionists always rejected this solution. They were backed by the Western powers and allowed to collect weapons and form a state within a state while the Palestinian liberation movement was disarmed. The fait accompli benefitted Zionist expansion. It is debatable whether in these circumstances the partition proposal was the best or the worst tactic for damage control. Note that the UN resolution for partition was accepted by all the Western countries and all of the socialist bloc of the time, but it was rejected by all the African and Asian countries. Perhaps the Soviets had broad tactical reasons for backing partition. The USSR was extremely isolated and was trying desperately to break the U.S. monopoly on nuclear weapons. The recruitment of Egyptian Communists to this tactic was debatable. The subsequent one-sided self-criticism seems to be an oversimplification of the situation in 1947 and 1948.

The Egyptian Communist movement has always taken an intelligent stand on Arab unity. It has never accepted the proposition of a multiplicity of so-called Arab nations and of state recognition as the goal of liberation. It has similarly never ignored regional differences much further in history than imperialist partition of the Arab world. It has never adopted idealist arguments of pan-Arab nationalism. The Egyptian (Wafd) and Sudanese (Umma) bourgeois nationalist movements clouded the character of Sudan. The Egyptian and Sudanese Communist movements defined a strategy of common struggle of two fraternal peoples against common external and internal enemies. Egypt and Syria formed a United Arab Republic in 1958 when progress in Arab unity seemed possible after the overthrow of the monarchy in Iraq. The Egyptian Communist movement did not hesitate to criticize the Nasser regime for its anti-democratic methods, which overlooked the specifics of the countries concerned. History has proved us right, as these methods were largely to blame for the failure of the union. Communist organizations on the ground took different stands, but the differences now seem marginal. The democratic movement for national liberation (Hadeto) held back its criticism of Nasser. The Egyptian Communist Party was more openly in support of the Iraqi prime minister of the time, Abdel Karim Kassem. In my view now, both positions were weak but fell within a broadly correct line.

From the time of the revival of Egyptian Communism (1942-1945) to the dissolution of the two parties in 1965 there was a multiplicity of Communist organizations. Violent personal disputes between the organizations prevented sober consideration of real differences in analysis and strategy. I now wonder if the search for unity (or the alternative of a "victory" snatched by one organization) was not the effect of the prevailing idea of the "party" as the sole and essential defender of the "correct line." A better approach to internal democracy within one or several parties would bring clearer debate without preventing a common front on many issues.

The multiplicity of organizations concealed a differing view of the broad revolutionary strategy on the historical agenda. For some national liberation came first. I may be stating this position in extreme terms but without wishing to be tendentious. According to this analysis, Egypt needed a democratic bourgeois national revolution. Others emphasized the need to move quickly from this phase to socialist construction. I do not think that the names of the various organizations can be pinned to the two lines, as they ran the gamut, even if the dogmatism of the time brought obscurity. Both sides cited as authorities the Soviet Union, Mao's *On New Democracy*, and so on. The ambiguities of debate and personality clashes worked against the brief unity in 1958, although we were happy to see it at the time.

The Free Officers' Coup of July 1952 and the emergence and evolution of Nasserism from 1955 to 1961 shifted the choice from the strategic to the immediate question: critical support or opposition to the new regime. Hindsight and a reexamination of the positions taken and the various justifications abound in the progressive Egyptian literature of today. It rarely grasps what I believe to be the essential point. Some activists in Hadeto argued that since they had been in the clandestine Free Officers' Organization, their party was better able to make a correct assessment of the progressive character of Nasserism from its birth. This does not seem to be the real issue.

Since 1960 I have argued that Nasser's program was essentially a bourgeois national proposal from the outset and never went any further. Its populist style did not contradict its content. It was the only possible way of implementing a bourgeois national proposal. The so-called liberal Egyptian national bourgeoisie was historically weak. Support of the popular classes was necessary and it was feared they would not fulfill the project (hence the stubborn anti-democratic side of Nasserism). The statist form of the proposal had nothing to do with the "transition to socialism," but was the only effective way to implement it. Unfortunately the strategic alliance between the Soviet Union and third world national liberation movements after Bandung, combined with the statism of the Soviet Union, had the broad effect of confusing statism and socialism.

With hindsight I believe that history has proved me right. Nasserism gave way to Sadatism, just as Brezhnev gave way to Yeltsin, although neither of these abrupt changes can be described as counterrevolution. I see them rather as an acceleration of the internal tendencies of the two systems. The new bourgeois class formed within and by statism is obliged to normalize its status. I have also said and written that in neither case was the evolution inevitable. A leftward evolution was possible, but it depended on a maturity of the socialist forces within these (and other) societies. In retrospect I feel quite comfortable in describing the bourgeois national project as utopian.

With this view I re-read the stands taken by the Egyptian Communist movement in a different way from the usual. I believe that Hadeto's critical support, sometimes challenged by the anticommunism of the authorities, was a fundamental mistake. It stemmed from the idea that a bourgeois national stage was essential and desirable and would be supplanted by socialism. My position is that actually existing capitalism as a polarizing world system makes any bourgeois plan essentially comprador. To deny this is to nurture the illusion of the bourgeois national utopia. I can now advance this position with greater clarity than thirty years ago, but I had an inkling even then.

I differ with the strong criticism that the Egyptian Communist Party, which I totally supported from 1950–1951, was fundamentally wrong about the character of the Nasserist proposal. The criticism has been shared by the Egyptian Communist Party since 1956 and is repeated ad nauseam today. It seems to me one-sided and coming out of a strategy that history has shown to be a failure. I leave aside secondary matters such as the "fascist" nature of the regime and possible imperialist complicity. Was it a mistake to see in the proposal a bourgeois plan doomed to failure?

The leftist position of the 1950s contrasted two alternatives: either a socialist revolution unbroken into stages or a bourgeois national revolution. I can now say that this antithetical approach came from an analysis, common to both options, that underestimated the polarization inherent in capitalist expansion. I can now say that Marxism was gradually stifled for failing to take this aspect into account. The social democrats seeking bourgeois revolution or the Leninist-Maoists seeking socialist revolution miss the real point. What is the character of revolution on the agenda when polarization makes both bourgeois revolution and socialist revolution out of the question?

I started my doctoral thesis in 1954, immediately after gaining the necessary higher diplomas. I did not have to hunt for a topic. I had long since decided to contribute to a Marxist analysis of the origins and course of "underdevelopment."

I had a clear idea of what I wanted to do: to examine the birth of underdevelopment and its implementation as a product of worldwide capitalist expansion—and not as a backward form of capitalist development. I chose as supervisor Maurice Byé. He and François Perroux responded favorably to my first outline and were always strongly supportive. They made detailed comments and encouraged me to be more precise while respecting my strong methodological choices.

I wrote the thesis fairly quickly and have maintained this habit. As I said above, I do not take the academic approach of an illusory quest for "perfection" sustained by an excess of footnotes. I prefer to be a militant whose writings aim to carry the debate forward. The work was well advanced in the autumn of 1955, and I virtually completed it in the first half of 1956. The Suez Canal was nationalized in July. Subsequent events, including the attack on Egypt in October, kept me fully occupied for a while, and I did not return to my manuscript until early 1957. I presented my thesis in June, married Isabelle in Paris in August, and returned to Egypt in September.

Without false modesty I may say that I am proud of my insights of the time. I had taken a position well ahead of its time. I argued that development and underdevelopment were two sides of the same coin: capitalist expansion. I chose a straightforward title for my thesis: "On the Origins of Underdevelopment: Capitalist Accumulation on a World Scale." For reasons of academic propriety my supervisor persuaded me to substitute a more esoteric title.[4]

Never before to my knowledge had underdevelopment been seen as a product of capitalism. The central idea was that an "underdeveloped" economy did not exist of itself but was an element in the world capitalist economy. The societies of the periphery were subjected to a constant structural adjustment (the very term used in my thesis) to the demands of capital accumulation on a world scale. In other words, there was no answer to polarization within the framework of capitalism. This was a new idea. The *desarrollismo* theory was just being formulated. The criticism by the so-called Latin American dependency school did not emerge until the late 1960s. The methodological hypothesis of the so-called world economy school was formulated still later, in the 1970s. The opposite theory—Rostow's "stages of economic growth"—was not formulated until several years after I had written my thesis. My thesis was, I believe, a prior critique of Rostow.

The thesis was a substantial text of 629 pages. I was constrained by the examination requirements, as I prefer brief syntheses without a display of the background material. It was expected that conclusions would be given statistical backing, although statistics do not reveal much. I was then a beginner unaccustomed to a strict choice of the truly significant facts. I also had to outline the positions I wished to criticize—a good student exercise no doubt, but an encumbrance on the final text. I wanted to link the particular arguments to the fundamental theories from which they derived. I decided to include a critical reading of conventional economics and the basic principles of the law of value, the system's dynamic of accumulation and reproduction, money, the business cycle, international exchange, and so on.

After the thesis was written I put it away in a drawer. Much later when the dependency school popularized the ideas that I had pioneered, I was invited to publish the thesis, and did so as *Accumulation à l'échelle mondiale* in 1970 (published in English by Monthly Review Press as *Accumulation on a World Scale*, 1974).[5]

In the subsequent chapters I shall consider in detail how my analysis of world capitalist polarization has evolved from my thesis to the present.

When I completed my doctorate I did not choose an academic career; instead I chose a political and social role.

I felt that endless inquiry into economic theory would not satisfy my broad intellectual interest in historical materialism. It would not meet my desire to put my knowledge into action. Later I shall explore the evolution of my thinking about historical materialism and the issue of socialism. Training as an economist gave me a good grounding. This is not always so for the many victims of the academic division of labor, which artificially separates economists from sociologists and historians.

We were entering a new historical era in the mid-1950s. It was an era of the triumphant ideology of development and a historic attempt to implement development policies in the third world. I returned to Egypt in 1957 to become involved in development administration at the precise moment when Nasserism was undergoing its first radicalization. My working life convinced me to challenge these policies. The debate on socialism was also entering a new phase, one that began with the crystallization of Maoism. The Twentieth Congress of the CPSU in 1956 was followed by the first veiled Chinese criticisms of Sovietism and the first formulations of their alternative road, marked by the Hundred Flowers movement in 1957 and the Great Leap Forward in 1958.

Later I shall return to Bandung period and relate it to my personal experience in Egypt (1957-1960), Mali (1960-1963), and then in the training and research institutions that gave me the opportunities to build on these lessons.

3

The Theory of Capital Accumulation: Its Formation and Evolution

THE FIRST PHASE: 1956–1970

In the discussion that follows, I outline my critique of economic theory as I presented it in my doctoral thesis of 1957 and in its subsequent published form in 1970.

Reading *Capital* had immediately persuaded me of the fundamental position of the Marxist law of value in the critique of bourgeois economics. To me it was not a question of a concept reduced to its positive aspect (the amount of socially necessary labor), as Ricardo posited it, but a critical holistic concept revealing the character of commodity alienation peculiar to capitalist society. Value determined not only capitalist economics, but all forms of social life in the system.

In response to Marx, an economic theory of value was constructed: the hypothesis of subjective value with objective laws of human economic behavior in the face of scarcity. It completely wiped out the essence of the capitalist system; namely, commodity alienation.[1] I noted that the subjective construct had no internal logic and was nothing more than a tautology devoid of real issues. I tried to offer an internal critique of neoclassical thinking. I stressed the failure of Böhm-Bawerk, whose concept of extending the production process did not allow the establishment of any productivity of capital distinct from that of labor and who was certainly obliged to assimilate the productivity of the capital in question to a supposed future depreciation that defined alienation.

The bourgeois economic theory incorrectly described as neoclassical opted for a static, or at best metastatic, method of analyzing the general equilibrium that eliminated continual accumulation as the driving force of capitalist life. Moreover, the combination of a subjective theory of value and the concept of general equilibrium entailed in turn an artificial and scientifically unsound quantitative theory of money.

I also offered a critical reading of Keynesianism within the framework described above. I showed that the Keynesian multiplier disappeared when it was considered that demand created supply only through intermediate investment. The multiplier is only meaningful if one replaces the concept of savings (available for investment) with that of hoarding (unavailable for investment). Keynes argued that liquidity preference set a lower limit on the rate of interest and that there was an insufficiency of investment at that minimum. I made the deduction that Keynes was a prisoner of monetary quantitativism. Keynes was certainly concerned about the real phenomenon of stagnation. The latter is the expression of the tendency of capitalism to create surplus productive capacity, since the wages and profit relationship (social distribution of income) tends to fall below the ultimate relationship between demand for consumer goods caused by wages and the demand for producer goods necessary to meet the ultimate demand. I had an explanation for stagnation without resorting to the monetary artifice of the interest rate.

The adoption of a dynamic outlook on capitalist expansion led necessarily to a confrontation with the position of "permanent stagnation" and the historical shortcomings of capitalism. I rejected the Ricardian and Malthusian positions based on diminishing returns. I had at the time accepted Marx's law of the tendency of the rate of profit to fall, but I later abandoned this. I tried, however, to explain the meaning through a critique of its expression in Keynes—the fall in the marginal efficiency of capital. I took the position that in the capitalist mode the deep continual and prevailing tendency was to create productive capacity above that of consumption capacity independent of any trend in the rate of profit. In 1966, Paul Baran and Paul Sweezy proposed their concept of "surplus" (a broader concept than that of surplus value, including nonproductive incomes and state revenues), whose absorption demanded rapid and increasing development of nonproductive expenditure.[2] I was prepared to accept this and thought highly of it.

In formulating a theory of accumulation in the capitalist mode of production, I diverged from Marx's schema, which was limited to the classical Department I (capital goods) and Department II (consumer goods). From 1973 I could forget the tendency of the rate of profit to fall and show the need for a growth in real wages as productivity improved in each department. However, wage improvement comes only when the social conditions of class struggle permit. The natural tendency of capitalism is to create a capacity to consume that is lower than the capacity to produce. The theory of accumulation that I articulated easily incorporates Baran and Sweezy's concept of surplus.

My aim was more ambitious, however. I sought to formulate a theory of accumulation on a world scale. This was not merely the theory of accumulation in the capitalist mode of production extended to the world scale. I thought it useful to begin with the embryonic critique of development theory derived from conventional economic theory. I drew the conclusion that the goal could be reached only by leaving the narrow framework of economics and rising to the level of historical materialism.

A Critique of Comparative Advantage

According to prevailing social and economic theory, the comparative advantage of the various partners in the world system was the motive for exchanges between them and a rational calculation justified the option for a development strategy open to the outside.

I had an insight that the two propositions were no more than the translation of an ideological prejudice and a damaging political option. I believed I had shown this to be so in my doctoral thesis. On this essential point I have nothing to add or withdraw. Although the Ricardian model balances comparative advantage, I noted that the gain from the exchange accrues only to the partner with an absolute advantage. From a dynamic point of view, the gains from improved production are greater than those from specialization based on comparative advantage.

If Ricardian and Marxist concepts of value were abandoned, the law of comparative costs no longer held. Instead a logical reconstruction of economic science was attempted on the basis of subjective value, or a positivist-empiricist approach was taken summing the returns from various productive factors. The argument fell into a vicious circle and rested on a hypothesis that simply assumed what it purported to show.

The Ricardian theory relied on presuppositions that the partners form segments of a capitalist mode of production operating on a world scale. Real wages are identical from one country to another, providing minimal subsistence, as with the gold price. I questioned if this line of reasoning was useful. I then realized that Marxism, which grew out of the prevailing nineteenth-century view that capitalism played its historic task of homogenizing the world on the basis of the capitalist mode, had shared the Ricardian perception. Bukharin's error that wage levels tend to equalize internationally was evidence.

I was back on track with what I saw as my essential contribution: namely, that capitalism as an actually existing world system is something more than the capitalist mode of production on a world scale. The absence of a theory of international trade in *Capital* was explained since Marx claimed—erroneously—that worldwide capitalist expansion would homogenize the globe as this expansion created a world market integrated in all its dimensions.

I noticed that adopting a dynamic approach had enabled Raul Prebisch to pinpoint the key issue in his early works, foreshadowing future positions on *desarrollismo* and then dependency. Technical progress was expressed at the centers of the system by a rise in real wages and on the peripheries by a fall in relative prices. I was only sorry that Prebisch, a positivist, did not go on to ask why this was so.

If comparative advantage did not explain the modern explosion of world exchanges, I had to look for a deeper explanation: capitalism's inherent tendency to expand markets. Only Marx and Schumpeter thought that this was significant and self-evident. I articulated the view that no contradiction exists between the tendency to build a world market for products and the parallel construction of a world market for capital, noting that all conventional economic theories were logically incapable of reconciling the two movements. In the construction of a world market for commodities and capital, underdeveloped economies— the peripheries—were subjected to continual structural adjustment to the demands of capital accumulation in the developed economies.

I took up the historic role and function of the periphery in world trade, distinguishing the period of Industrial Revolution (1800-1950) from that of mercantilist capitalism, when exchanges were distinct from the long-distance trade of earlier phases. The depression Marx saw was marked by wretched wages in the new industrial centers and hence equal exchange and relative marginalization of exchanges between center and periphery. I pursued Prebisch's observation, mentioned earlier, that the terms of trade did not worsen in the peripheries until about 1880, when the wage gap between the center and the periphery began to widen. I attached vital significance to the break represented by imperialism in Lenin's definition.

In 1969, Arghiri Emmanuel reopened the debate with his theory of unequal exchange.[3] I drew my own conclusions: wages grew along with productivity at the center but not at the periphery. This meant a deterioration of the double factorial terms of trade and the transfer of value on a world scale, described as unequal exchange.

In asserting capitalism's inherent tendency to expand markets, I came up against the matter of outlets. I took the position that I still hold: dynamic accumulation requires no external outlet other than that provided in the abstract framework of the capitalist mode of production. I criticized Rosa Luxemburg's position and countered with the argument that accumulation merely required an active role for credit. I was not blind to the history of conquest and peripheralization of noncapitalist areas as new fields for capitalist expansion. I could see what the reconquest of the East and industrialization of the third world could mean in the future. I related it to the depression Marx saw in the mid-nineteenth century, when Europe turned inward in its Industrial Revolution. If Marx underestimated the significance of the polarization inherent in accumulation on a world scale, it was perhaps for reasons peculiar to a fairly brief moment in the history of capitalist expansion.

A CRITIQUE OF THE THEORY OF MONEY

I began with a complete rejection of the quantitative approach in post-Ricardian bourgeois theories. I argued that, contrary to what neoclassical economists later asserted, Ricardo was not a crude quantitativist. My critique was based on what I described as the passive role of credit—namely, adjusting supply to demand—which even Keynes had failed to see. By contrast, economists of the anti-quantitativist tradition, such as Charles Rist, had (along with Marx) always highlighted this.

Britain was on the gold standard before 1914. This not only stabilized prices but also lowered prices in the long run through improved productivity. The tendency was countered as productivity in gold production rose through exploitation of U.S. deposits in the mid-nineteenth century and South African deposits at the end of the nineteenth century.

On this basis I made a critique of Nikolai Kondratieff's theory of so-called long cycles. Coming off the gold standard created a situation where credit could exceed needs and ended the concept of a normal level of prices. This is desirable and functional for monopoly capitalism. Inflation (as a notion distinct from price increases) is impossible on the gold standard, but it becomes a policy that is systematically exercised in and beneficial to new forms of competition between monopolies. This means coming off the gold standard.

The prevailing ideology presents the relative prices of capitalism as an expression of market rationality, but the description is wrong. As Leon Walras understood, rationality would demand free movement of capital—namely, the abolition of any scope for self-financing and in turn the abolition of private property. I observed later that Soviet reformers from the Khrushchev era onward proposed just this utopia of capitalism without capitalists.

Money and credit do not play only this passive role, important though it is. On the basis of Rosa Luxemburg's critique, I showed that the dynamic of accumulation demanded a corresponding injection of credit: this is the "active" role of credit that I described as the regulatory mode.

A CRITIQUE OF THE CYCLE THEORY

The cycle is not a monetary phenomenon but the periodic expression of the imbalance between production capacity and consumption capacity that is specific to capitalism—a continual tendency to imbalance that is continually corrected. I proposed a self-generating model of a cycle based exclusively on the concepts developed in *Capital* in the modern accelerator-multiplier terminology. I added to the model the factors of credit, real movement in wages, and the rate of profit, without reducing the cycle to a monetary form. I offered a critique of modern bourgeois theories in Roy Harrod, John Hicks, and others.

We were encountering in the phase after World War II new modes of regulation, later described as Fordism, that could even out the regular deep fluctuations of the extended nineteenth century (1800-1950) and replace them with a pattern of shorter periods and less deep fluctuations.

A CRITIQUE OF THE THEORY OF EQUILIBRIUM IN THE BALANCE OF PAYMENTS

The underlying concern of all conventional methods of economic analysis is to legitimize the capitalist system by trying to show that it is governed by self-regulatory mechanisms which tend to restore equilibrium and thereby provide optimum satisfaction. This concern is particularly apparent in the theories of external balance of payments that they all use to show that market forces tend toward equilibrium. The propositions seemed to me unscientific. In my thesis I described this desperate quest as an expression of the "ideology of universal harmonies."

I considered in turn three suggested modes of automatic regulation: price effects (ignoring anomalous elasticities), exchange effects (another form it takes), and income effects (which merely tend toward equilibrium and are similar to those of the law of outlets).

I restored these analyses to the framework of a gold standard, then the special form of gold exchange standard and fluctuating rates, noting that going off the gold standard meant an end to fixed exchange rates. The quest for equilibrium in exchange rates entailed an unscientific quantitativist monetary theory, as Albert Aftalion had seen. The quest had also failed to define the mechanisms through which such rates could be secured. Instead of fantastic ideas such as Joan Robinson's artificial invention of equilibrium in exchange rates ensuring full employment, I offered the concept of a dominant exchange rate ensuring a distribution of returns consistent with the structural adjustment of the weakest nations to the worldwide expansion of capitalism. I proposed to shift the analytical terrain to take into account the true mechanisms that tended to restore a measure of equilibrium, through what I called structural adjustment of the weakest to the strongest.

A CRITIQUE OF EMERGING DEVELOPMENT THEORY

Development theory was only emerging at the time. I wanted to show at the outset that it was doomed to failure, as can be seen today in the crisis of development theory.[4] I chose the analytical tools of conventional economics but offered a critique of their internal logic. I considered the false problems they raised in monetary mechanisms and anomalous situations. I showed that their considerations on disequilibrium in the external balance of the periphery justly described as persistent led necessarily to abandoning conventional tools for a systematic analysis of structural adjustment in the periphery to the demands of worldwide accumulation. This analysis leads out from the narrow field of economics to the broader field of historical materialism.

I tried to show the inconsistency of propositions on money management by newly independent countries seeking to use them as a development tool. I argued that the issue of credit in the dependent countries based on the gold exchange standard played the same role as in the centers. The critique I made of exchange theory (in price, exchange, and income effects) seemed valid in all cases in the periphery as at the center; there were no anomalies peculiar to peripheral systems. I drew attention to the need to shift analysis from these false problems to the real problem: banking integration of the peripheral systems for structural adjustment. The plea for monetary independence must be part of an escape from the jaws of international integration. It was essential to go the whole way and to abandon the illusion of free trade; this was evident in the failure of independent currencies in nineteenth-century Latin America. It was essential to withdraw from banking integration and institutional exchange control.

I noted a second group of false problems in the much-discussed transmission from the centers to the peripheries. The transmission was seen in quantitative monetary mechanisms or the external trade multiplier. I felt obliged to analyze the problems of a global capitalist crisis. The cycle provides a means of structural adjustment to the demands of worldwide accumulation. From this perspective, the economies at the periphery do not appear as poorly developed and dependent segments of a world system but as overseas extensions of the central economies. The peripheries played a significant role in the worldwide expansion of capital. They allowed recovery of exports from the centers by speeding the break-up of the non-capitalist or precapitalist environments. I suggested that the analyses must reflect the specifics of successive phases in the globalization process. I recalled the essential role of the peripheries in the colonial era. I noted the changes after 1945 as the modernization of Europe became the center of gravity in the new phase of worldwide accumulation. I suggested even that industrialization of the third world and incorporation of the countries of Eastern Europe could in the future play an essential part in the quest for the worldwide expansion of capital.

The pressure exerted by this structural adjustment underlies the persistent tendency at the periphery to a deficit in the external balance of payments. Pressure on the external balance of payments always follows the continual progression of absolute advantage benefiting the centers; the limited range of products available in the periphery; the pressure for repatriation of profits; and the social impact of worldwide polarization in urbanization, inequalities of income distribution, increase in administrative costs, and so on.

I included in this analysis what I called the transfer of the multiplier effect of investment (the combined effect of the multiplier and the accelerator) from the peripheries to the centers of the system, produced by the strong marginal propensity of the peripheries to import and export the profits of foreign capital. I further deduced that the underdeveloped economy was not a backward local economy but a limb of the dominant economy.

I criticized Prebisch's explanation of the twentieth-century periphery's persistent deficit in the external balance of payments. Prebisch compared the United States' weak propensity to import with the strong propensity of nineteenth-century Britain to import. I noted that it was a peculiar effect of the rebuilding of Europe and Japan. Once this was achieved, the United States would be obliged to open up to foreign exports.

In analyzing the negative balance of payments of the peripheries I drew a rare, but still significant, distinction between the balance on real account (where the impact of the unbalancing forces imposing structural adjustment is seen) and the balance of bank capital movements associated with banking integration. The two entities are frequently confused, especially by the International Monetary Fund (IMF). This avoids the genuine problems of structural adjustment and substitutes false problems, such as self-regulating market mechanisms. The system provides no solution for the asymmetrical situation of persistent structural deficit in the peripheries. In nine cases out of ten, devaluation leads to price increases that cancel it out. It is a matter of a world transmission belt for price structures, meaning that the world monetary system serves accumulation on a world scale. A model of a developed capitalist economy could be conceived without including international relations, but this method is meaningless for an economy on the periphery. The notion of autocentrism becomes decisive.

I began the analysis of structural adjustment by bringing together a series of issues generally considered separately in economic analysis.

Monetarization of sectors of the subsistence economy and sectors inherited from previous precapitalist modes through external assault (imports) creates a crisis by leading to the ruination of craftsmanship, which operates now for the benefit of foreign rather than local industry. This generates new forms of oppressive and exploited production, later labeled the "informal economy."

The subsequent flow of foreign investment in mining and export cash crops entails a repatriation of profits in excess of investment. Peripheral growth takes on the uneven form of miraculous hopes suddenly dashed. The periphery's absence of autonomy is stressed; it becomes merely an overseas segment of the center economy. I argued that the flow of foreign investment in the peripheries differed from investment in new centers. These new centers moved up gradually in position from new borrowers to mature borrowers to lenders, while the peripheries were trapped in the second phase and were eventually pushed back into the first.

The overall dynamic of accumulation on the periphery is governed by exports, whereas in the more articulated centers, production of the means of production is linked to production of goods for local consumption. I linked the driving force of production for export to the increasing inequality of income distribution in the periphery. This brought to light a whole range of distortions as symptoms of modern underdevelopment, including impoverishment of the peasants and enhancement of the position of land-owners; preference for investment in light industry; markedly low wages in relation to productivity; disarticulation of the economy; and the juxtaposition of economic "miracles" with areas of devastation.

The conventional tools of neoclassical economics did not allow a correct analysis of these issues. In the debate on the most rapid development of the tertiary sector, disparate activities were jumbled up, as I showed in my thesis. I found more useful the classical debate of Adam Smith (and the Marxists) on the distinction between productive and unproductive labor, with the former engaged by capital in the process of production and the latter collecting income for service. In the debate on the rationality of investment choice, neoclassical economics was lost after Böhm-Bawerk, who, as I said earlier, was unable to establish a concept of the productivity of capital other than that of future depreciation. The debate on rationality of economic choices lost its essence: that the share of consumption and investment is the effect of a social relationship (expressed as distribution of income between wages and profits) and could be replaced by another collective rationality.

The critique of emerging development theory made in my doctoral thesis was dated by the time it was published. The polarization between industrialized centers and non-industrialized peripheries was at a turning point, and a new phase of industrialization was taking place on the periphery. The examples and historical experiences on which I based my analyses belonged by force of circumstance to the worldwide polarization that was on the way out. In a summary of the analysis, I shall say more of the limits imposed by this objective context.

THEORY AND HISTORY

The critique of emerging development theory was based on its apparent root in bourgeois social thought which accorded primacy to economics and was lacking in logical rigor. I was led naturally to analyzing underdevelopment in terms of historical materialism. I did not regard this as the tacking on of various aspects arising from separate disciplines, as happened in some schools of bourgeois thought. I saw it as a unity of history and theory, and of the economic, political, and ideological domains.

It was natural for me to reject cultural and demographic theories of underdevelopment just as I had rejected the economic explanation in conventional economics. I did not pay much heed to these developments beyond the formal needs of the thesis. I noted merely that the demographic explanation lacked rigor. Its concept of optimal population was meaningless without an awareness of modes of production (the productive forces and relations of production). It did not tell the true demographic history, namely, that the demographic revolution of capitalism, and of European peoples before it, affected others. I must add that demography has not made any progress in persuading me of the opposite but has remained apart from the theory of capitalism, accumulation, and proletarianization.

I thought that the building of a theory of accumulation on a world scale required a theoretical history of social formations. I formulated the requirements in the opening pages of my thesis. I noted that integration into capitalist globalization had led to an original development of capitalism in the peripheries, which meant that under-development could not be regarded as a prior phase of development. Because theory and history should not be separated, I had to reflect on the dynamic of systems beyond the dynamic within the system.

My first conclusions were formulated in the following propositions:

(1). The genesis of underdevelopment is outside the conventionally defined field of economics. The unity of analysis required here—the world system and not the national formations that compose it—entails defining on a world scale the bourgeoisie as well as the productive classes subjected to exploitation.

(2). Polarization between centers and peripheries is defined as a differential in rewards for labor. Rewards are lower in the periphery than at the center for equal productivity. The results of industrialization of the peripheries must be revalued in that frame.

(3). Political phenomena, such as working-class social democracy in the centers and Leninist ideas prevailing in the peripheries, were meaningless outside a framework of social polarization on a world scale produced by capitalist accumulation on the same scale.

(4). The construction of a theory of formations of actually existing capitalism was delayed by the vulgarization of

Marxism, whereby the economic base was seen as having the same determinative effect in capitalism as in previous modes of production. This vulgarization destroys Marx's fundamental discovery of the specific character of capitalism, namely, economistic alienation.

On these foundations I suggested a historical approach derived from recognition of basic modes of production (primitive community associated with the ideology of kinship, as I described it at the time; the slave mode; the feudal mode and its cousin the tributary mode; the simple commodity mode). They were successive or overlapping, and sometimes embroiled in broader groupings through long-distance trade.

When it came to the peripheral capitalist formations, I refused to discuss them in terms of a dualism, or juxtaposition of modernity and former traces. I suggested a classification based on the history of their integration into worldwide capitalism. My propositions rightly stressed the predominance of agrarian and mercantilist capitalism, which are now, some thirty years later, being overtaken by new forms of polarization. I saw that the peripheral bourgeoisie is naturally from the beginning and under any forms of polarization a "comprador" class with national ambitions that go no further than trivial autonomy. State capitalism was at the time still on the ascent in the radical nationalist regimes of the third world. I did not regard it as the beginning of a transition toward socialism but as a new form of the worldwide expansion of capitalism.

SUMMARY

The position I held in 1957 was certainly ahead of its time. This was clear even from the references in the title to the structural effects of the international integration of precapitalist economies and the mechanisms engendering the so-called underdeveloped economies.

From then on I argued that underdevelopment was not a backward phase of development but a modern phenomenon of worldwide capitalist expansion responsible at the same time for the development of the centers and the underdevelopment of the peripheries. I borrowed the terms "center" and "periphery" from the early writings of Prebisch but gave them a new content. Rostow's position was economistic, mechanistic, and simplistic, like so much of bourgeois ideology (hence its success). He popularized a linear, evolutionist view but was as yet unpublished and did not appear until 1960. A critique unfolded in the late 1960s. The work of the Latin American school was just beginning, and Raul Prebisch had not yet formulated the *desarrollismo* that I regarded as an evolutionist formula, although he showed much more finesse than the crude propositions made by Rostow. In the 1960s and 1970s *desarrollismo*, later known as "dependency theory," became the typical development ideology among the third world ruling classes of the Bandung project. *Desarrollismo* was subject to a leftist critique, which I think did not go to the heart of the matter. I adopted the Maoist critique when it emerged in the early 1960s and especially from the beginning of the Cultural Revolution in 1966. The method I proposed in 1957 of regarding the world system as the framework for an analysis of accumulation preceded the formation of the world system analysis school of thought.

I argued from the outset that underdevelopment was produced by the structural adjustment of societies that were not in on the beginning of the qualitative leap represented by the constitution of the national bourgeois state and an autocentric capitalist economy on that basis. The societies were subjected to the external expansion of the bourgeois states. I stressed the fundamental distinction to be made between peripheries and new centers. They have a different social dynamic. In brief, rewards for labor in the centers keep pace with productivity, but this is not the case in the periphery. Underdevelopment is not a passing phenomenon, but the effect of the logic of accumulation on a world scale. The law of accumulation and pauperization operate on this scale and not in the centers treated artificially in isolation. Polarization is not an accident attributable to specific local causes in culture or demography or elsewhere. It is inseparable from actually existing capitalism and cannot be avoided in the framework of the logic of capitalist implementation.

My critique of ideology did go to the heart of the matter. I drew the logical conclusion that a genuine development policy implied control over external relations—in other words, delinking—without which the attempt at internal structural reform was doomed to failure.

I did not belong to what the World Bank dubbed the pioneers of development. I was rather among the pioneers of the *critique* of development. This has become almost fashionable today, since the patient is dead.

Even so, the formulations I offered from 1957 to 1970 were far from adequate. I shall go on to consider shortcomings and mistakes that I addressed in the later years.

My demonstration entailed a fundamental critique of bourgeois social thought, especially the pseudo-scientific economics constructed in response to the historical materialism originated by Marx. I was seeking to show the logical incoherence of so-called neoclassical economic science. I concluded that there was no point in specializing in this useless, bothersome, and absurd hodgepodge and engaging in an endless critique of it. The subsequent efforts of economists to develop a methodology to turn their science into a management tool of the capitalist system have not always been in vain—from their point of view. I have never been sufficiently interested to make a personal contribution.

The analysis of the economic aspect of reality as I grasped it when I was writing my doctoral thesis did not later on seem to me totally convincing and adequate. On some issues I was trapped in a literal or erroneous interpretation of my reading of Marx.

The Chinese Cultural Revolution was a key moment in my perception of these shortcomings. The revolution occurred between the presentation of my thesis in 1957 and its initial publication in 1970.

Maoism criticized the Soviet experience from a leftist perspective, as opposed to the rightist critique offered by reformists since the Khrushchev era. I believe it was not wrong to say, in the language of Rossana Rossanda and the Italian *Manifesto* group at the time, that it was a return to Marx, which had been gradually watered down by Sovietism and prior to that by the European labor movement to which Sovietism was heir. Maoism called for a consideration of the transition and a reharmonizing of its contradictory goals. Should one catch up by giving priority to developing productive forces, even if that meant reproducing many of the essential features of capitalism, or should one build an alternative society? The debate that was at last open posed the issue of the non-neutrality of technology, which had been missing previously from historical Marxism. On this point I made the appropriate self-criticism and exposition. Underlying the conflict between catching up and building an alternative was a more fundamental debate on the significance and extent of polarization in actually existing worldwide capitalism. This was the issue I always considered and was central to my doctoral thesis.

Marxist political economy as I grasped it was insufficiently aware of this polarization. I submit as evidence my view of pauperization attributable to accumulation in the capitalist mode of production. I adopted Lenin's position that accumulation (in the abstract model of the capitalist mode) does not entail a growth in real wages, as the market may be expanded (indefinitely?) through the demand for producer goods. I broke with this schema in 1973. I concluded that extended reproduction in the abstract framework of the general schema of the capitalist mode of production entailed a growth in real wages. Similarly I abandoned the theory of the falling rate of profit. This shift forced me to take the issue of polarization further and to reformulate it later as the law of accumulation on a world scale and the pauperization through which it is made manifest on the same scale.

In the subsequent years I sought to reformulate the law of accumulation on a world scale by distinguishing it more sharply from accumulation in the capitalist mode. This concern led to a reassessment of the periodization of capitalism in the past, present, and likely future.

In my doctoral thesis and in *Accumulation on a World Scale* I attached great importance to the emergence of monopoly capitalism in 1880. I believe that Lenin's insight is rooted in and confirmed by the evolution of the capitalist system to the present. His analytical approach on this issue is far superior to that of radical left-wing economists who reject Marxist-Leninist propositions on imperialism. I tried to show their inconsistency in my critique of the positions of E. H. Chamberlin, Joan Robinson, and Michael Kalecki. The later contribution of Baran and Sweezy further convinced me that the transformation of capitalism in the age of monopolies was significant.

The propositions in my doctoral thesis about the periodization of earlier phases were also revived as my concept of polarization was sharpened.

A new phase began with the industrialization of the periphery, but this was embryonic in the 1950s. The new features must be re-examined in a critical spirit, but with an understanding that the Bandung era was only just beginning. Even so I addressed the period with enough doubt about the character of the project to be unsurprised later by its speedy suffocation. Further evidence came in the studies I made in the 1960s of some of these experiences (Nasser's Egypt; African socialism in Mali, Guinea, and Ghana; neocolonialism in the the Ivory Coast and the Maghreb).

By abandoning economics I was able to explore the potential of historical materialism. The concern in the later years enabled me, I think, to do the following:

- Formulate the law of globalized value in a form that was not spelled out in the doctoral thesis.
- Specify the character of the historical contrast between the tributary mode and capitalist mode, and reformulate the theory of the relationship between the economic base and the ideological and political superstructure.
- Propose a thesis of unequal development on a historical scale.
- Bring into the framework a critique of the ideology of capitalism, especially in its Eurocentric cultural aspect.

When I was writing my doctoral thesis it was hardly possible to make a serious analysis of the Soviet system because its economist ideology and practice were largely unknown. From the end of the 1950s, the Maoist critique was able to go further than the superficial Trotskyist critique of worker power distorted by bureaucracy. From then on I ceased to regard Soviet society as socialist (distorted or not) and saw it as a new reality of its own kind. I criticized the priority given to catching up. I made a contribution to launching debate on the worldwide aspect of socialism.

THE SECOND PHASE: 1970–1990

In my doctoral thesis in the mid-1950s I had reached conclusions to which I have remained attached and regard as definitive:

(1). Underdevelopment is not a backward phase of development but a modern phenomenon of worldwide capitalist expansion initially polarizing and shaping the distinction between centers and peripheries by continual structural adjustment of the peripheries to the demands of worldwide expansion of capital which dominates the centers.

(2). The analytical framework for all the major problems of society that gradually reached modernity after 1492 is the world system and not the local and national social formations that compose it.

(3). The world system is based on the capitalist mode of production whose logic overturns the order of previous dispensations and is expressed in economistic alienation. This means that the law of value dominates not only economic life (which becomes autonomous) but all other aspects of social life (which become subject to it).

(4). Bourgeois economic science ignored the specific character of capitalism from the outset. It had no genuine scientific foundation; it was tautological and nothing more than an ideology used to legitimize the system and avoid the real issues.

(5). Bourgeois economic policy based on this so-called science was at best the art of managing capitalist expansion and effective only in some circumstances.

(6). The development policies pursued in this spirit were always ineffective and could never achieve the stated goal of reducing the North-South gap.

I pointed out the inadequacies of these analyses in my writings in the years from 1955 to 1965, in the still confused formulation of the distinction between the law of value in general and the law of worldwide value as the foundation of polarization.

In the years from 1965 to 1972 I concentrated on elucidating the concept of the law of value worldwide. This meant explaining the mode of operation of capitalism's economic laws (above all the law of value) in terms that incorporated the holistic method of historical materialism. I believe I achieved much of my goal in the formulations in three of my books: *L'Échange inégal et la loi de la valeur* (1973); *L'Impérialisme et le développement inégal* (1976) and *La Loi de la valeur et le matérialisme historique* (1977), all of which were translated into English.[5] The following discussion is based on these three works.

To advance the analysis of capitalist polarization, I continually reconsidered its history in the light of concepts of worldwide value. The period we were in was precisely that of a new stage of globalization based on unequal industrialization of the peripheries, the result of changes brought about by the rising tide of national liberation. I sought to review my early formulations, which were too closely tied to the previous phase of polarization. I made a detailed analysis of the new "development experiences" and situated them within the evolution of the world system.

Using an analysis based on historical materialism, I examined:

- The law of value in the capitalist mode of production.
- The distribution of surplus value in the capitalist world.
- The law of worldwide value operating in a polarized world system.
- The law of value in the capitalist mode of production.

I always accepted the centrality of the Marxist concept of value because economistic alienation is peculiar to the capitalist mode, defining modernity. I rejected the alternative posited by Piero Sraffa in *Production of Commodities by Means of Commodities* (1960). This analysis was warmly welcomed on the left as the method that avoided the tautological rubbish of the subjective value of the neoclassical schools. I commented merely that the so-called neo-Ricardian method remained descriptive. Like all alienated economics thinking, it continued to formulate economic laws as if they could be objective necessities independent of social struggles.

My holistic approach, which I believe was at the heart of the historical materialist method, made me take an opposite view: that class struggle does not reveal the "necessary economic equilibrium," but determines one possible equilibrium among others. What were these struggles? I suggested three levels: the capitalist mode of production at its highest level of abstraction; historical national social formations; and the world capitalist system.

I set out to reformulate the first level. The explanation of the dynamic of accumulation within a schema reduced to Marx's two departments led me to the significant conclusion that the system demanded an increase in real wages in relation to the productivities in each department. Based on this general conclusion, I made certain additional observations:

(1). Credit plays an active role in the process of realization of the product.

(2). The system has an inherent tendency to over-produce.

(3). As stated by Baran and Sweezy in *Monopoly Capital*, it may be possible to pursue accumulation without sufficient growth in wages through absorption of surplus in a third department.

(4). Schemas of dynamic accumulation were necessarily constructed on the hypotheses of given technologies. These hypotheses canceled the dialectic between objective forces and subjective forces and wrongly perceived technology as neutral regarding social relations. I formulated the dialectic as: the class struggle operates on an economic base and shapes the way this base is transformed within the framework of the immanent laws of the capitalist mode.

(5). The impact of technology on social relations has deeper implications in education and technology. Similarly, the study of productive forces must include the dimension of nature. This dimension was rediscovered at a conference on the environment held in Stockholm in 1972. I doubted capitalism's ability to incorporate nature into its economic calculations.

(6). The model of dynamic accumulation meant abandoning the falling rate of profit and analyzing its fluctuations in practical historical terms.

(7). Reintegration of the law of value into historical materialism was inspired by the renewed critique of Soviet economism launched by Maoism.

The reason for abandoning the Marxist concept of value was because it was supposedly impossible to transform values into prices. I noted that this impossibility contradicted the argument that the rates of profit as calculated in the price system and/or in the value system were equal. The two rates had to be different, because if they were not the system of labor exploitation would be transparent, as it was in systems before capitalism. The argument against transformation revealed an economistic interpretation typical of "Marxian economics." It ignored the specific character of commodity alienation that gives the concept of value its genuine significance. I was inspired by the pioneering work of Beaudelot, Establet, and Toisier in *Qui travaille pour qui?* [Who works for whom?] (1979) and spelled out my argument in *L'Économie arabe contemporaine* (1980), where I pointed out the implications for the Arab economy of the distribution of total direct and indirect labor incorporated in various final products.[7]

THE DISTRIBUTION OF SURPLUS VALUE
AND HISTORICAL MATERIALISM

In addition to the production of surplus value and its transformation into profits, Marx planned to do a historical materialist analysis of distribution through the intervention of social forces. I refer to the unwritten books of *Capital*, which Marx entitled "Landed Property," "The State," "Foreign Trade," and "World Market and Crises." Issues raised by the first item had in part been discussed in volume 3 of *Capital*, and the crises were discussed in volume 2. I had already stated in my doctoral thesis the reasons why, in my view, Marx gave up dealing with international economic relations, as the pre-Marxist bourgeois economics of Ricardo had done and post-Marxist neoclassical economics was to do. Indeed, these issues (the state, foreign trade, the world market) were not situated in the domain strictly defined by the capitalist mode of production. I later recalled my early insight.[8]

Only a shift of the analysis from the level of the capitalist mode of production to that of the social formation permits a consideration of the secondary distribution of surplus value between profit, interest, and rent.

I pursued the consideration of interest begun in my doctoral thesis in my critique of the theory of money. I rejected the superficial view that the rate of interest was determined by supply and demand for money, as if two subunits of capitalists—lenders and financial borrowers— were face to face in the market. I accepted Marx's basic proposition that the supply of credit adjusted to the demand (demand creates a supply and the market is false). I looked at the role of the banking system as collective agent of capitalism. Like the state, the system regulated accumulation, according to the very term I use, by operating on the cycle and in the field of international competition. In 1992, I wrote a systematic presentation of the issue in an article on regulation. In a recent reconsideration of *Monopoly Capital* in the December 1991 issue of *Monthly Review*, Sweezy also returned to this issue of the distinction between the real economy and the financial economy and their interaction.

I tackled the question of ground rent in a critique of Marx's explanation in volume 3 of *Capital*, where he determined the absolute rent by the differential between the organic compositions in agriculture and industry. I sought to examine rent as a category of distribution, with the landowner not intervening in the process of production. The real issue is whether the conflict between landowners and capitalists operates on a given economic base and changes it. I discussed the matter in particular historical terms relevant to Britain, France, and so on.

Consideration will be given below to other aspects of the distribution of surplus value, especially regarding the distinction between formal submission and real submission drawn by Marx in his analysis of the integration of petty commodity producers, particularly peasants, in the economic system of the national capitalist formation or regarding mining rent.

Historical materialist analysis prevents a separation of the operation and extended reproduction of the capitalist economy from the social conflicts modifying the economic base. I criticized the alternative answers provided by so-called radical (non-Marxist) analyses of historical capitalism (for example, the political economy of multinationals), pointing out that history and theory are inseparable. I went on treating them as a unity operating on the scale of a world system and not of national formations treated in comparative isolation.

LAW OF WORLDWIDE VALUE

The notion of worldwide value presented in my doctoral thesis was the central axis of my book *L'Échange inégal et la loi de la valeur.* I transferred my conclusion on the relation between the value of the labor force and the development of the productive forces in the capitalist mode of production to the level of the world system. I urged that the value of the labor force was determined at that level and not in the local formations that composed it. However, the labor force has different prices at the center and at the periphery (where its value is constituted by a weighted average) because of the varying social conditions created by the worldwide expansion of capital.

I defined the world system as dominated by the globalization of value and argued that unequal exchange was only the tip of the iceberg. I explained the concept of polarization: differences in rewards for labor greater than those characteristic of productivity.

I put forward the hypothesis that the center-periphery distinction fell entirely within this schema. Dependency was only a manifestation of the center-periphery polarization. My analysis posited a world system founded on a market that integrated commodities and capital and excluded labor, whereas the concept of the capitalist mode of production supposed a market that integrated all three.

Bukharin's error, doubtless shared by Marx, was to underestimate the central significance of this distinction between the capitalist mode of production and the world capitalist system. I therefore rejected Bettelheim's proposition, noting that "If we follow Bettelheim in accepting that wages are autonomously determined in each social formation, we can no longer have a theory of international trade. We must then accept Ricardo's theory of comparative advantages." Bukharin's hypothesis was based on "the triple international mobility of goods, capital, and labor." Under imperialism "the mobility of commodities and capital leaves the national space to embrace the whole world while the labor force remains enclosed within a national framework" and one is faced with a problem of distribution of surplus value on a world scale. I strongly rejected the accusations of circulationism brought by dogmatic interpreters of Marxism at the time.

I note here that in 1973 I did not date the true constitution of a world system (with mobility for commodities and capital) to before the formation of monopoly capitalism in Lenin's meaning, namely about 1880. When I returned later to an analysis of the phases of formation and evolution of the system I felt bound to introduce refinements into my analysis.

The theory of accumulation on a world scale formulated in the way I still regard as definitive showed that "Unity has never been synonymous with homogeneity." The schemas of value transfer (a term synonymous with world distribution of surplus value) proposed on the basis of globalized value at once brought in a range of issues whose analysis belongs to the field of historical materialism.

Transfer (concealed in the price structure) goes from the noncommodity (subsistence) producers or simple commodity (peasant) producers to the capitalist producers (capital yielding profit or wage labor enabling price to be above value). I was able to take in the issues of exploitation of domestic labor, especially of women, and of formal, nonreal submission of peasants in the worldwide genesis of surplus value. These were certainly issues that arose in the central and peripheral formations. I illustrated them with a schema that proposed that at the quantitative level these mechanisms yielded worldwide polarization between centers and peripheries.[9]

The worldwide unity of the system means that collective surplus value is generated at this level, and this was what anticirculationist prejudice failed to understand. I found totally acceptable Michel Beaud's observation that the recent evolution of the system engendered a worldwide productive system that replaced the former national productive systems and a more markedly worldwide character in the generation of surplus value.

The center-periphery distinction could be expressed in two contrasting schemas. The schema for the center revolved around Marx's two departments. The typical scheme for the periphery revolved around production for export and luxury consumption.[10] The distinction is not removed by new industrialization at the periphery or by globalization of the productive systems since the involvement of Marx's two departments is also to be found on a world scale.

The unity of the world system transfers the matter of pauperization to this level. The increasingly wider polarization in per capita income is an undeniable fact. It is explained by the objective circumstances of class struggle at a world level operating on the objective basis of polarization. For this reason I insisted on analyzing the class structure, and the conflicts and alliances that form around it, on a world scale. I also insisted on the geographical separation between the active and passive reserve army, a point I reinforced in a recent debate with Giovanni Arrighi.[11] In *Delinking* I sketched out a schema of pauperization on a world scale by drawing out the Lorenz curves of income distribution in the core capitalist and rural peripheries of the system.[12]

The theory of mining rent also finds a natural place in the analytical approach I offered. Mining rent, in contrast to agricultural rent, concerns a nonrenewable resource whose cost (in capitalist calculation) is limited by the time prospect of calculation of profit, whereas for the community this cost is quite different. I suggested analyzing mining rent in precise historical terms. From a capitalist point of view, the rationale for mining rent is the level at which the rate of profit is maximized on the world scale through reestablishing equivalence between supply and expanding demand by enlarging the mass of labor exploited. I brought in a historical periodization linked to the world division of labor. In the old form of polarization based on nonindustrialized peripheries, property rent was reduced to the minimum required for the alliance between capital and local proprietors. In the new form of polarization associated with industrialization, land rents are less important and are transferred to the profit of world and local capital, while the conflict over mining rents becomes more acute. I therefore wrote, "Mining rent emerged because Algeria and Iran are industrializing themselves (even if only in a dependent way), and not the reverse." I added the appropriate comments on substitutes in this theory of rent.

I explained my position on a world capitalist law of value in the contrast I drew between its reproduction model, the Soviet statist model, and a reproduction model from a delinked popular national outlook, in *The Future of Maoism*.[13]

I went deeper into the concept of globalized value in the debate on unequal exchange launched by the appearance in 1969 of Arghiri Emmanuel's book on the subject.

In this debate I retained the concept of double factorial terms of trade I had advanced in my doctoral thesis, because the concept included the relationship between productivity and the rewards for labor. I defined unequal exchange on this basis. I went further than Emmanuel and rejected anything reflecting logically necessary demands for an analysis in terms of comparative advantage. I rejected, for example, that international exchanges referred to "specific" products. I had to respond to one obvious objection. Why is it that capital does not migrate in large quantities to the periphery, where it can profit from higher rates of exploitation of labor? My answer was that on a world scale equilibrium between global supply and demand would be broken in favor of massive overproduction that could find no outlet. I therefore propounded a schema of general equilibrium on a world scale created by distribution of productivity and costs of labor power. This led from the tip of the iceberg of the concept of unequal exchange to that of structural adjustment of the peripheries and the unequal world division of labor through which it was made manifest, thereby bringing equilibrium in the balance of payments. I continued the analysis in my recent discussion of Emmanuel's position on the new phase of globalization and reproduction of polarization by the "aristocratic monopolies" of the centers.

I retain my original thesis on unequal exchange in the narrow sense, that it was a latecomer with imperialism. I shall consider refinements in a subsequent chapter on the history of capitalism and its successive phases.

4

The Globalization of Capital: Center-Periphery Polarization

In Chapter 3 I traced the formative steps of my theory of accumulation on a world scale. I concluded that polarization is inherent in the worldwide expansion of capitalism. It has occurred throughout its five centuries of history—from 1492 to the present day—and will continue for the future so long as the world remains organized on capitalist principles. I concluded further that polarization worsens from one period to the next; it is the most strikingly explosive aspect of the history of actually existing capitalism and its most tragic historical boundary. Two further boundaries indicated by Marx are inherent in the fundamental logic of the capitalist mode of production. They are alienation of the human being, who is reduced to a commodity labor power; and destruction of the natural basis of reproduction.

Polarization shows that history and theory are inseparable. It explains why the prevailing conventional social thinking has no scientific value: it refuses to accord polarization a central place in analysis of the system and treats it as an epiphenomenon of specific local circumstances. Such a theory is a constant feature of the discourse of power and its heralds: it is possible to catch up without challenging the principles of capitalism, merely by making intelligent use of them to join the globalization. One can imagine a World Bank expert traveling in the Americas of the seventeenth century hailing the "miracle of Santo Domingo" and ridiculing the choice of the New England settlers to construct a self-reliant economy. He could not for an instant have imagined that the miracle would turn into what Haiti has become, and that the poor wretches of New England would produce the United States. At every moment of history the "good pupils" are pointed out. We all know that today it is South Korea and other newly industrializing countries (NICs). What will become of this language if, as I argue, the new industrialization of the periphery increases polarization in the future we are building? We can bet that the defenders of globalization and the opponents of the delinking option will not be self-critical. The World Bank played a significant role in drafting the development policies of the 1960s and 1970s—policies that could lead only to the catastrophe we see today—a point that I was making at the time. There will not be one word of self-criticism from the World Bank.

In this chapter I hope to give an overview of the history of world capitalism that I have gradually come to see it, not as a complement to the theory of accumulation but as an essential component of accumulation.

I was faced with a long list of historical issues: the mercantilist period from the sixteenth to the eighteenth century; the role of the Americas in this phase; the conflict among the European powers and the problems of successive hegemonies in modern world history; the status of the English, American, and French bourgeois revolutions; the Industrial Revolution; Kondratieff's theory of long cycles; the nature of the break at the end of the nineteenth century described by Lenin as the passage to monopoly capitalism and imperialism; the colonial phenomenon; and the transformations that paved the way for the new globalization of capital.

This chapter addresses these issues. The reading of history I propose entails a critical parallel reading of the strategies developed by antisystemic forces that, knowingly or not, are in conflict with the logic of capitalism operating at various levels. It entails a critique of the development theories and practices implemented after World War II, theories that I have continually studied from 1955 to 1992 (see also Chapter 6). The critique leads to alternative proposals, which I will discuss in subsequent chapters.

PHASES IN THE EVOLUTION OF WORLD CAPITALISM

There is a strong tendency to read history as continuous development, with each step preparing for the next. This method tends to diminish the impact of moments of rupture and accelerated or abrupt change, especially social, political, technological, and ideological revolutions. It instead draws attention to their long incubation and the marginal effects of the changes they bring, because the real outcomes of such revolutions are never what their authors expected. Revolutions are stifled and the past takes it revenge.

At their most extreme, optimists regard the history of humankind as a slow unfolding of "progress" (or Progress), whereas pessimists view it as an endless desperate attempt at a fresh start. This wipes out the specific character of the successive phases: of capitalism in comparison to the previous systems and of the project for a future socialism. I rejected the historical viewpoint of Andre Gunder Frank, for example, because I found it evasive and thought it negated the qualitative change introduced by capitalism.[1] I always insisted on the need to identify the specific character of each successive moment in history. I attached special significance to moments of qualitative transformation—that is, to revolutions—and have particularly considered the significance of the French, Russian, and Chinese revolutions.[2]

I gave special note to four turning points:

- 1500: the concomitant birth of capitalism and of modern polarization produced by European conquest of the globe.
- 1800: the end of the mercantilist transition, industrialization, and the crystallization of the capitalist mode of production in its fully fledged form, and the French revolution.
- 1880: the transformation of capitalism into monopoly capitalism.
- 1990: the end of the postwar era, the end of Sovietism, and the dawn of a new phase of globalization.

I have rounded out dates to avoid secondary issues on the precise dating of each qualitative change.

There are three phases between the dates indicated:

- 1500-1800: mercantilist transition.
- 1800-1880: competitive capitalism.
- 1880-1990: original monopoly capitalism.

No phase can be analyzed in exclusively economic terms, but must be seen at the broader level of historical materialism. The turning points indicated are not the only significant dates in modern history. Varying periodization will follow for varying viewpoints on modern history, for example, the possible unfolding of Kondratieff's long cycles, or hegemonic succession. Attention must be paid to moments of intense technological innovation, to political and social revolution (the Russian Revolution of 1917, the birth of the People's Republic of China in 1949), to the ebb and flow of revolt on the periphery (colonization of the Americas, 1500-1800; colonization in the age of imperialism, 1880-1950; decolonization, 1950-1970; forcing the periphery into a comprador role, from 1980).

I shall try to trace the formative steps of my theory of polarization inherent in world capitalism. I shall show the links between the broad phases and other modalities of the periodization. Within the context of the formation of peripheral capitalism, I shall consider what is at stake in the contemporary crisis of the global system.

The periodization at which I arrived, gradually in some respects, entailed particular responses to general theoretical questions, especially on mercantilist transition, the character of the change from competitive capitalism to monopoly capitalism, long cycles, and hegemonic succession.

In my doctoral thesis I was already treating the colonization of the Americas and the accompanying mercantilism as the first turning point or chapter of capitalism. I explained this view in the panorama of peripheral formations I put forward, where I noted the particularly significant role of the American peripheries for primitive accumulation in Atlantic Europe as a prelude to the Industrial Revolution.[3]

I arrived at this particular historical periodization by focusing on the relationship between changes that took place in European society and the American peripheries in the three centuries of mercantilism (1500-1800), and the transformations that took place within European feudalism (and elsewhere) after 1500.

On the former I took a stand in the great debate opened by Maurice Dobb, Kohachiro Takahashi, and Paul Sweezy.[4] My first position was that the internal transformations of feudalism and Atlantic mercantilism were mutually reinforcing. I was not really happy with this conclusion, as I thought—and still think—that the internal transformations of feudalism and the birth of new capitalist relations within it were neither new nor peculiar. They emerged in 1500 but dated back several centuries in Europe itself. Similar evolutions were in operation, sometimes over centuries, in other, non-European societies. I did not find a satisfactory answer until later, when I formulated the specific character of feudalism as the peripheral form of the tributary mode of production.[5] Feudalism at the periphery was flexible in comparison to the rigid fully fledged tributary forms in China and the Islamic world. The internal transformations had greater potential in Europe for accelerated development and a qualitative leap, especially in the organization of power and its social content. (I shall return to this significant issue in "A Note on Historical Materialism.")

This new and unambiguous formulation of the link between internal and external factors led me to give decisive weight to the acceleration of capitalism brought by mercantilist exploitation of the American periphery.[6]

I had, of course, to insist on the specific character of the mercantilist transition and distinguish it qualitatively from previous moments in feudal Europe and in the Italian cities (1200-1500) and from parallel moments elsewhere (for example, Islam in its first glory, 800-1200; China during the Ming dynasty, 1368-1644). In the previous moments, the conflict between the developing protocapitalist forms and the logics of the tributary power (or its feudal peripheral expression) express a general law, namely the contradiction general to all (and not merely European) tributary societies between the objective demands of the development of productive forces and the renewal of relations of production. Hence I kept the description of "transition to capitalism" for the period of European mercantilism (1500-1800) and refused to apply it earlier or elsewhere.[7] I drew an analogy in the conflict between embryonic capitalism and the tributary forms operating in feudal Europe and in other tributary societies in the Orient. This ties in with my critique of Eurocentrism and its manifestation in historical materialism, in the guise of "two roads" (European and Asiatic) or "five stages." I shall return to these issues in "A Note on Historical Materialism."

The Industrial Revolution is a second decisive turning point. Capitalism fully fledged in the capitalist mode of production entailed not only wage labor but also crystallization of capital in significant industrial plants that are themselves the product of social labor. It is only then that the law of value takes full effect on the basis of a three-dimensional integrated market (commodity goods, labor, and capital). Mechanized industry (as opposed to the manufacture of the mercantilist age) is needed if one is to speak of the capitalist mode of production in its full meaning. It is only then that the real scope of the specific characteristics of capitalism that I stressed (commodity alienation and the predominance of economistic ideology, exponential growth, widespread urbanization, and so on) becomes apparent.[8]

The Industrial Revolution inaugurated a dramatic increase in polarization between 1800 and 1950. Center and periphery became virtually synonymous with industrialized and nonindustrialized regions. The latter were gradually integrated into the international division of labor as agricultural and mineral exporters. At the same time, the Industrial Revolution gave the industrialized countries overwhelming military superiority, which enabled them to make a cheap conquest of the world.

As we know, the Industrial Revolution began in Britain at the end of the eighteenth century. During the period of France's revolutionary and postrevolutionary wars, it spread throughout northwestern Europe and to New England. It spread east and south in Europe during the first half of the nineteenth century. Central Europe rapidly caught up (from 1850 to 1870), while Japan was the last country to reproduce the model.

But why did this revolution take place in Britain before it did in France, its main rival in the mercantilist epoch? The prevailing explanation is that the answer lies in the internal dynamic of English society: in the agricultural revolution and the political democracy inaugurated by the 1688 revolution. I agree with Immanuel Wallerstein's minority view that Britain had minor and dubious advantages in the

agricultural revolution and the area of technological innovation. I see how Britain benefitted from its direct and
indirect colonial exploitation of the Americas. I agree that
it was this dominant position in the center-periphery
relations of the time that gave Britain the advantage over
its competitors in the implementation of the Industrial
Revolution.

The emergence of monopoly capitalism at the end of the
nineteenth century is a third turning point in the history
of the worldwide expansion of capitalism.

Lenin, as we know, stressed new forms of competition
between national oligopolies that dominated the national
productive systems of the main centers and pointed out
that their conflict in economic and international political
fields inevitably led to war. Conventional economics, with
its intricate treatment of oligopolistic competition, has
never really considered the profound effects of monopoly
on the economic, social, and political structures of the
centers. The main contribution in this field is that of Baran
and Sweezy, who suggested the concept of absorption of
surplus appropriate to monopoly capital.

Lenin drew a close link between the colonial
phenomenon and monopoly imperialism. There is no
doubt about colonial expansion at the end of the
nineteenth century. However, colonialism was not new. I
insisted that there must be no confusion between the
concept of expansionism—a constant feature inherent in
capitalism from the outset that had shaped the imbalance
between the center and the periphery before 1800—and the
concept of imperialism in the age of monopolies.[9]

From the point of view of the periphery, what was new?
I argued in Chapter 3 that unequal exchange emerged after
1880, for only from that date did wages in the centers keep
pace with productivity. The previous period was marked
by stagnation, or even reductions, in real wages, and the
gap between wages and productivity had been a source of

accelerated accumulation that explains the speed with which the Industrial Revolution transformed the European and North American landscape within a half-century. The transformation broke down the internal anti-worker social alliances of the bourgeoisie and paved the way for a new social compromise between capital and labor as the basis for new growth in wages.[10]

The new system of regulation—analyzed by Lenin in political terms as the emergence of a labor aristocracy—has the complementary aspect of unequal exchange between the industrialized centers and the agricultural and mining peripheries.

The previous relations between center and periphery were not equal, with or without unequal exchange. I noted that America in the mercantilist era did not in fact "trade" with Atlantic Europe, but that its production was shaped totally to serve the accumulation of mercantilist capital.[11] This explains why it was precisely the regions such as New England—which were not organized in this way, but delinked and unincorporated from the exploitative system of the time—that were later able to make prodigious leaps in development. These were the "young centers" that turned into the axis of the modern world system. After the Industrial Revolution, the peripheries were shaped as suppliers of agricultural and mineral products. Prices of these products were controlled in such a way as to keep down capital costs at the center. These prices did not stem from the economic law of free-market competition but were the result of systematic policies. More will be said in the section on peripheral capitalist formations. As always, the center-periphery distinction was not the result of market laws, since the market is shaped through the polarization by transnational and local alliances that provide the basis for the structural adjustment to which the peripheries are subjected.

I noted, however, that Marx's work came at a time when

the Industrial Revolution was spreading in Europe, and center-periphery relations were less important than they had been in the past or were to be again. I think this is why Marx relegated primitive accumulation to precapitalist history, underestimated polarization, and proposed a law of pauperization in general without clarifying that in fact this law operates at a world level but not at a level of centers artificially separated from the global system.

We seem to be returning to a system similar in some ways to that of Marx's time. Globalization has been increasing in recent years principally through the interpenetration of the central economies marginalizing the fourth world periphery, but further integrating other NICs into the world market for commodities and capital.[12] Without a concomitant worldwide labor market, the NICs will become the true peripheries of tomorrow. The fourth world may be somewhat marginalized in economic aspects, but this is only temporary. For all these reasons, I argue that 1990 represents a new turning point in the history of capitalism.

No social phenomenon, or even perhaps a natural one, develops in a regular, constant, and unending manner. The same must be true of capitalist expansion, whose phases of rapid growth are inevitably followed by moments of difficult readjustment. Therefore the reader of history is left with an impression of evolution through long waves. But acknowledging a phased succession does not mean necessarily adopting the cycle theory. It is possible to speak meaningfully of a cycle only if a specified mechanism reproduces the movement with monotonous regularity.

In narrowly defined conventional economics (of production, investment, prices, and incomes), long waves can be noted. Price indexes showed a tendency to fall from 1815 to 1850, rise from 1850 to 1865, fall from 1865 to 1900, and rise from 1900 to 1914. The explanation I gave has nothing to do with the cycle theory. But the turning point dates of

1850 and 1900 correspond to the exploitation of rich new gold deposits in North America and then in South Africa. I argued that in a monetary system based on gold (as happened from 1815 to 1914), the evolution of absolute prices was determined by a prolonged tendency to fall, through improved labor productivity. This tendency is countered by subsequent improvement in labor productivity in gold production. This was dramatically the case in 1850 and 1900, with the opening of exceptional new deposits, and the effect of the consequent rise in prices was exhausted within fifteen years, leaving the prolonged tendency to fall to resume its sway.

No cycle theory is required to consider the effect of long cycles on rates of production growth, to which investment is bound to be closely linked. Each expansionary phase is matched by major innovations and political evolutions to expand markets: the first Industrial Revolution and the revolutionary and Empire wars; the railway and German and Italian unification; European and Japanese reconstruction; the age of the motor car and the Cold War.

I do not side with Trotsky in his polemic against Kondratieff. Trotsky thought the innovations, exploitation of new resources, wars, and external expansion, and even the effects of class struggle, were outside the causal field of a theory of the economic cycle. He artificially separated political economy from the broader field of historical materialism. In my view, Kondratieff had the acute insight that historical materialism made it necessary to link narrowly economic phenomena and changes in other fields of social reality. I argue with Kondratieff that these aspects of reality are also expressions of capital accumulation. However, their relationship does not support any cycle theory.

I have always thought it nonsensical to project before 1800—let alone before 1500—a theory of long cycles that incorporates an anachronism. The specific contradictions of the capitalist mode were obviously not to be found in previous periods. It is, for example, absurd to talk of a tendency to overproduction in these periods.[13]

There is also a strong tendency to read the history of capitalism as a hegemonic succession, dating from 1500 in some accounts and 1350 in others. I find none of these propositions persuasive for the modern period, let alone for the earlier times. They contribute nothing to an analysis based on the concepts of historical materialism.[14]

The world system school has generally tilted the balance too far in favor of its own principle, namely the determination of the parts (the states) by the whole (the world economy). My approach led me to refine the answers on hegemonies that are successive but dissimilar. First, supposed hegemony in the capitalist world economy was not worldwide hegemony. From the sixteenth to the nineteenth century the world was not reduced to Europe and its American appendage. To say that Venice or the Netherlands was "hegemonic" does not make sense in terms of the scale of the time. Even at the scale of the European capitalist world economy that was being formed in the three centuries of mercantilism, I do not understand how Venice or the Netherlands can be described as "hegemonic." They were certainly remarkable commercial and financial centers, but highly constrained to cope with the feudal world surrounding them on all sides and with the consequent political balances, through the conflict of the great monarchies. The Treaty of Westphalia in 1648 did not enshrine a Dutch hegemony, but rather a European balance to cancel it out.

I doubt whether one can even speak of British hegemony in the eighteenth century. England had control of the seas, to the detriment of its French rival. It was not yet capable of asserting particular authority in the affairs of continental Europe, or truly to dominate the potential overseas peripheries. Hegemony came much later, with the opening of China and the Ottoman Empire after 1840 and the quelling of the Indian Mutiny in 1857-1858. Britain's industrial advance and financial monopoly, though substantial, did not bring true hegemony. The so-called world hegemony was constrained by the balance of power in Europe, in which Britain did not dominate. No sooner was the hegemony of Britain in place (1850-1860) than it was challenged by the industrial and military rise after 1880 of its rivals, Germany and the United States—even if London did retain a privileged financial position long after that time.

I concluded that hegemony was far from being the rule in the history of worldwide capitalist expansion, but rather a short-term and frail exception. The system generally was ruled by enduring rivalry.

Have things changed since? Are they really changing now? U.S. hegemony after 1945 was in some ways quite new. For the first time in the history of humankind, the United States had the military means to intervene (through destruction and genocide) on a global scale. The United States was held back from 1945 to 1990 by a military bipolarity shared with the USSR. The United States is by way of becoming what nobody has been before, except Hitler in his imagination: military master of the world. But for how long?

Regarding long cycles, I have always rejected suggestions of projecting the phenomenon of hegemony backward, as wiping out the specific character of capitalism in comparison with the previous tributary systems.[15]

The periodization of modern history cannot be reduced to its economic aspect, even if it is extended to the political competition between powers on international terrain. I have always insisted on evolution and qualitative changes in the social and political aspects of social reproduction.[16]

I attach great importance to ideology and have commented on the decisive role played by the three great revolutions of the modern world—French, Russian, and Chinese.

POLARIZATION AND SOCIAL FORMATIONS IN PERIPHERAL CAPITALISM

I suggested summarizing the center-periphery distinction in a two-fold schema. One part involved the articulation of production of capital goods and consumer goods in a self-reliant capitalist economy. The other part involved the articulation of exports and luxury consumption in a peripheral social formation.[17] Although this is an old theme, I showed that the peripheral articulation applied not only to the phase of capitalism marked by the absence of industries at the periphery but also to the new phase of third world industrialization. The conventional debate was over import substitution versus export industries. The World Bank, for example, was embroiled in this. But as I stated frequently, it begged the question of industrialization for self-reliance, meaning industry at the service of the agricultural revolution. The industrialization could have an outward look and bring interdependence in the real meaning of the word, not an unbalanced dependence. I stressed the link between the new phase of polarization I could glimpse, when industrialization of the periphery was only beginning, and the internal social polarization, peculiar to the peripheries, and translation to a world scale of the laws of accumulation and pauperization.

This schema was not an abstract theoretical invention. It was the abstraction of what I could discern from careful analysis of the social formations on the capitalist periphery, especially in my Arab and African case studies or from my readings about American and Asian formations. I shall return to this key point, illustrating the method I adopted of going from the concrete to the abstract. The schema is a skeleton on which the muscle of these social formations could be modeled.

My approach placed polarization and the theory of worldwide capitalist expansion at the center of history. It was inevitable that I would take an interest in the constitution and evolution of peripheral formations and their specific character in relation to central formations. My analysis was first published in *Accumulation on a World Scale* and continued in *Unequal Development*, whose subtitle, *An Essay on the Social Formation of Peripheral Capitalism*, showed that my intention was to go beyond the bounds of economics into the field of historical materialism.

There is no need for me to deal at length here with analyses that I have not modified except in minor details. I drew my conclusions on the American formations from the Latin American school (Fernando Henrique Cardoso, Darcy Ribeiro, Andre Gunder Frank, Celso Furtado, Aníbal Quijano, and so on). I note the original shaping of American formations at the outset, the pseudo-feudal and slave forms becoming meaningful only in relation to their subjection to mercantilist capitalism; the domination of nonfeudal *latifundia* agrarian capitalism in the states emerging from independence and the alliance between this dominant class and British imperialism; the critique in this framework of *desarrollismo*, as an expression of the thrust of a new industrial bourgeoisie. In my view, the latter accepted incorporation in the world system and could only replicate and widen polarization and be speedily stifled. (I wrote this when *desarrollismo* was at its height.)[18]

I was quick to see the significance of third world industrialization and the new forms of reorganization of the world system it was bound to bring. I would go further in saying that I regard 1990 as a fourth turning point in capitalist expansion, and possibly as significant as the previous ones. Latin American industrialization began earlier, and I hypothesized that the crisis of the 1930s and the industrial populism that came in answer to the challenge was the beginning of a qualitatively new turning point.[19]

I wrote about Arab, Asian, and African formations on the basis of case studies I had carried out in the 1960s in Egypt, the Maghreb, and sub-Saharan Africa.[20] I set out some of my conclusions systematically in various articles.[21]

The questions that arose and the answers suggested for the Arab world gave a foretaste of my later writing.[22] I highlighted analysis of the specific character of precapitalist Arab formations (matters of long-distance trade, the renaissance of Islam and Nahda, etc.). My analysis showed that the transformation of landed property was a new way of integrating *latifundia* capitalism into the world system—not a vestige of feudalism, as was commonly argued at the time. I suggested a reading of Egyptian history from 1800 as a series of successive abortive attempts at autonomous capitalist development. This shaped my assessment of the Wafd as a liberal bourgeois party (which I could not describe as national in the Marxist sense of the word at the time) and of Nasser's regime.

For sub-Saharan Africa I suggested a reading that went back to the slave trade and its retrograde effects. I analyzed the Oriental mercantilism associated with Mohamed Ali's policy for Sudan, the history of Zanzibar, etc. I went back to the attempt to adapt to new international trade in the period before colonization (1800–1880). I remember arguing my position on the three forms of colonial exploitation in Africa and on the emergence of agrarian capitalism and its circumstances.[23] I completed the analysis of the shaping of African formations with a critique of neocolonialism and the European Economic Community (EEC) policies of prolonging the nonindustrialization of Africa after 1960, thus paving the way for the subsequent fourth world.

I drew four conclusions from my analysis. (1) Agrarian capitalism—not vestiges of feudalism—predominated. (2) A bourgeoisie that was by nature comprador, and not "national," was formed in the wake of imperialism. (3) Bureaucratization peculiar to the contemporary periphery occurred and launched a new phase of polarization based on peripheral industrialization which replicated and widened internal social polarization. (4) Proletarianization was incomplete at the periphery and created a socially marginalized reserve army of labor on a world scale.

I also considered the "new centers" in the framework of global European expansion by self-reliant societies (delinked from the structural dependence dictated by the logic of polarization and not to be confused with the peripheries).

What I sought to do in *Unequal Development* was to synthesize the theory of accumulation (an incomplete formulation, as I showed in Chapter 3) and the distinction between central and peripheral social formations so that the world system could be examined as a coherent capitalist system on a world scale. I addressed significant issues of the transition to capitalism, such as the freezing of tributary formations and long-distance trade and the concept of nation (more on this in "A Note on Historical Materialism").

THE CONTEMPORARY CRISIS AND THE FUTURE OF WORLD CAPITALISM

The capitalist logic of the world system always demands examination of any disequilibrium between supply and demand at the appropriate scale, whether the disequilibrium is momentary and passing or structural and lasting.

For structural crises in the contemporary world, the scale is the world system itself. Dysfunction in the globalized law of value is manifest in overproduction on a world scale caused by inadequate distribution of income at this scale.

Any crisis is a shining example of capitalism's inherent tendency to overproduction. It can be overcome only if at the scale of the system where it is operating there are social and political mechanisms forcing appropriate redistribution against the spontaneous tendency of capital. These regulatory mechanisms imply state intervention. That is why it takes so long to overcome structural crises, since there is no international regulatory system. The crisis is overcome only at the end of prolonged exploratory structural adjustments. The outcome depends on the resolution of local and international social and political conflicts.

The current crisis dates back to the early 1970s—even before the first oil price increase of 1973. Income redistribution on a world scale in favor of the peoples of the periphery would have provided a solution to the crisis. Hence, the New International Economic Order (NIEO) proposed by the nonaligned nations in 1975 was perfectly rational from an abstract point of view. As there is no world political system that plays the role that the state plays in the national context, however, the rational solution was rejected by the dominant countries and not imposed. From the start of the proposed NIEO, I analyzed its vicissitudes as deceptive proposals for Keynesianism on a world scale.[24]

The crisis provides an opportunity to shift the burden onto the weaker partners, namely, the peripheries. This aggravates the crisis. It contains a latent conflict between the social forces within the imperialist bloc (combining the social bloc at the center, so long as it does not break with imperialism, with the subordinate local comprador blocs of the periphery) and the anti-comprador social forces at the periphery. There would be greater hope of emerging from the crisis if there were an international alliance between workers in the developed capitalist countries (abandoning their solidarity with "their" national capital) and the anti-comprador bloc in the periphery.

We are far from this. The weakening of the working class and historic left stance in the centers encourages capital to take a so-called neoliberal hard line that is manifest in an increasing inequity in income distribution. As globalization spreads to the centers in the United States, Europe, and Japan, in the absence of shared regulatory mechanisms, the crisis can only be aggravated by competition among them.

Since 1978, this has been my methodological framework for analyzing the crisis of development, its contradictions, the policies pursued, and my own suggestions for action.

When I was writing my doctoral thesis, the third world had not yet embarked on industrialization. Its social formations were generally characterized by the predominance of an agrarian ruling class as a transmission belt for imperialist domination. I was well aware that this order would be overthrown, not, as bourgeois ideology continues to assert, by the natural effect of economic evolution, but by the intervention of an active agent for change, the national liberation movement.

According to my analysis, the imperialist phase was made up of three successive periods. The first was triumphal expansion until 1914, marked by an alliance with the agrarian bourgeoisie and the first generation of the mercantilist comprador bourgeoisie. In the second period, the expansion was challenged by a long series of anti-imperialist uprisings, including Mexico after 1910, China after 1911, Turkey and Egypt after 1919, the Russian Revolution in 1917, and the Chinese Revolution from 1927 to 1949. In broader terms, a challenge came from the modern national liberation movements after World War II, in the Indian Congress, Latin American populism, and so on.

During the 1950s a third period emerged. Third world industrialization began under the leadership of its bourgeoisies and caused a readjustment in the world system. I criticized the view of the Third International, which was too ready to see the period between the two world wars as a "general crisis of capitalism." It underestimated the new renewal of capitalist expansion that led to third world industrialization. I criticized the embryonic Sovietism that would later describe this development as the "noncapitalist road."[25]

I drew attention to the rise of U.S. hegemony, whose plan to rebuild the world market entailed an alliance with the new bourgeoisies against the old colonialisms. Commenting on the new industrialization, I concluded: "Henceforth, the peripheral bourgeoisie is strategically in the capitalist camp, even if tactically some of its fractions may, according to local circumstances, be anti-imperialist."[26]

I added that the inevitably unequal industrialization would atomize the unity of the third world into "sub-imperialisms" (though I criticized the terminology and suggested that the new peripheries be treated as imperialist runners) and "abandoned areas" (later called the fourth world) as a foretaste to the later "discovery" of differentiation within the third world.

I suggested that this kind of industrialization, whether private, classic, or statist, would speedily be stifled by external pressures and internal shortcomings and contradictions. I thought that 1968 marked the end of short-term illusions.[27] Two possibilities emerged: an aggravation of the center-periphery polarization, renewed with accentuated differentiation within the third world, or the emergence of a new wave of popular struggles, which was then possible to imagine because of the Marxist renaissance inspired by Maoism.

I analyzed the NIEO proposal as the swan song of the Bandung period begun in 1955 with the bourgeois national project for interdependent modernization and industrialization. The attempt to reorganize the world system was supposed to give a second wind to this development.[28] I later made a systematic presentation of this view of the period and project.[29] I had meanwhile taken part in numerous debates on the future of the project and the supposed delinking experiences by radical African, Arab and other third world governments that called themselves socialist. (I doubted if it had been delinking.) I was not surprised that the attempts were numerous. I was not surprised either that the easy adjustment to the world system of the peripheries in the expansion period from 1948 to 1968 should become difficult in the time of crisis. It seemed to me that the objective difficulties of the project had always been underestimated, especially in Africa.[30]

The global crisis was overt after the late 1960s. In the early 1970s I was among the minority (with Paul Sweezy, Harry Magdoff, Giovanni Arrighi, Andre Gunder Frank, and Immanuel Wallerstein) who, even before the oil price increase of 1973, described this as a structural crisis. More than twenty years later, the conventional economists and governments continue to use the language of "short-term crisis" and talk of recession and recovery.[31]

Between 1973 and 1990, which marked the end of this period, I tried to analyze the various aspects of the global crisis: the internal crisis of the peripheral societies and the crisis in North-South relations; the relationship of this crisis to the developing crisis in the North (competition between the United States, Japan, and the EEC; a declining America); and the evolution of East-West relations.

In 1973, I was still toying with the possibility that a revision in North-South relations would give a second wind to industrialization, especially in the statist countries.[32] From 1974, I believed that the initiative had gone to the Northern camp. In 1984, the North, according to the logic of its system, imposed on the third world the option of subordinate industry, marginalization, or a mixture of the two, accentuating differences within the third world.[33]

Andre Gunder Frank and I referred to George Orwell's *1984* and helped bring it back from obscurity. The continually increasing centralization of capital seemed to me to lead inexorably to a statist capitalism, of which Japan was perhaps already giving an example in efficient competition with other countries.[34] I also expressed anxieties about the decay of Western democracy, with references to Herbert Marcuse's *One-Dimensional Man,* functional reality, and media-induced uniformity. I suggested that Soviet statism, although primitive in form, might represent a strong trend for the future. Statism, as the negation of the fragmentation of capital, brought into question the law of value. I referred to Robert Fossaert's concept of development value and the expunging or mutation of the law of value that the spread of automation entailed. The progress of the Soviet collapse and the triumph of liberal anti-state ideology seemed to go the other way. I then noted that the latter success was not sustainable and therefore merely temporary.[35] I shall return to these issues in the discussion on the prospects for socialism.

I noted that capital's plans encountered numerous obstacles. The U.S. alliance with the South in the 1973 oil price increase was a U.S. counteroffensive in the competition with Europe and Japan. But it was difficult to find a real solution to the crisis. One possibility was the integration of Eastern Europe. The USSR, despite its military power and particular ideology, had the characteristics of a "sub-imperialism." On the other hand, the frailty of southern Europe was a weak link in the chain. The European left was strong at the time, but it was vacillating. While there might be a revival of social democracy, I was afraid of the authoritarian neoliberal option of a German Europe.[36] There were ideological obstacles to the revival of a left response to the crisis: the ideology of necessary adaptation to the development of the productive forces, imperialist behavior, the economism of "state collectivism."[37]

I addressed these issues in *Class and Nation, Historically and in the Current Crisis* (1980), and contrasted the imperialist plan to encourage comprador roles with the plan of the smothered bourgeoisie of the South. I expected a greater capacity to resist, a determination to restore a southern front through South-South cooperation, and more effective Soviet support. It seemed to me that the Soviet ruling class still hoped to be reintegrated into the system as a genuine central national bourgeoisie and not as a comprador peripheral bourgeoisie.[38] I returned later to the mediocre results of these efforts, particularly in the fields of energy, technology, agriculture, and cooperation.[39]

In my contribution to *Dynamics of Global Crisis*, I suggested a systematic history of the course of the crisis: the ideological crisis in 1968; the dollar crisis in 1971; the oil price increase in 1973; the U.S. defeat in Vietnam in 1975. I addressed the conflicts in southern Europe and the right-wing stabilization of these countries that had once seemed to me weak links offering the left a potential for revival. I considered the U.S. decline against a fragile European unity riven by the threat of Germany going it alone, arguing that "any analysis of economic rise and fall that centers on technological breakthroughs ignores that it is not techniques that count, but the social capacity to implement them." I stressed the U.S. military advantage: "There is no doubt that the sphere in which the United States can react most efficiently is the military one."[40]

Doubtless at the time I overestimated the chances of a speedy response from the people in the South (what I called a popular national response, inspired by the struggles in Nicaragua and South Africa). The bourgeois national project seemed well and truly stifled and incapable of resuscitation, as the "noncapitalist direction" did not seem a realistic alternative.[41]

I suggested an open-ended analysis of the Soviet strategy in crisis: the Soviet bourgeoisie in refusing peripheralization might slide into military adventure, but there seemed to me "new perspectives for the development of the socialist movement in the East and West."[42] It was necessary to avoid the dilemma of a Chile or Afghanistan.

The various forces still seemed fluid and the regional stabilization projects frail. I did not succumb to the fashion of overestimating the rise of Japan. I stressed the frailty of an East Asia bloc as long as relations with China were not settled. Similarly, I stressed the constant danger of a crash, with unpredictable consequences but possibly including an increased demand for "statism."[43]

As the crisis worsened in sub-Saharan Africa, it became a fourth world. I had always believed this was caused by Africa's maintenance of colonial structures through the EEC association with the African, Caribbean, and Pacific countries. This made it impossible to intensify agriculture and the supporting industrialization.[44]

I have always tried to set responses to the crisis within the context of immediate international events.[45] I always analyzed capital's offensive as aimed mainly at restoring the South to a comprador role, using NATO to reduce competition among the Western countries, and manipulating conflict with the East to prolong U.S. hegemony. I noted that the success of this offensive depended on the peoples of the East and South. Would they stand idly by?

The years from 1988 to 1992 were marked by an acceleration of change that marks the definitive end of the postwar phase. Some issues that were still open are now settled. The end of the Soviet cycle brings radical change to internal relations and to the prospects for the internal evolution of societies throughout the world. I questioned whether the system of Soviet statism was "stabilized" or "in transition."[46] History has settled the matter.

The collapse of the USSR ends seventy years of hostility from the Western powers toward a state that once threatened to build a socialist alternative. The hostility was expressed through wars of intervention, Hitler's aggression, and the Cold War. Nothing has been settled by the collapse. The peoples of Eastern Europe and the former USSR are condemned to peripheralization and will be forced to deal with the unenviable fate capitalism reserves for them.

The collapse of the bourgeois national project in the peripheries has occasioned an ideological offensive whose purpose is to have us believe that there is no alternative to integration into the capitalist expansion. It is a return to bourgeois ideology of which I have already made both a general critique and a particular one in the case of Korea.[47] This collapse, which is linked to the failure of the development ideology associated with the Bandung project, leaves a void that has not yet been filled with a national, popular, and democratic alternative; it has also not addressed the new challenges, such as the environmental crisis (which I will discuss in Chapter 5). By default, polarization will increase. Far from narrowing it, third world industrialization will only widen the gap. The putting-out model of industrialization subordinates the peripheral societies and subjects them to orders from the centers dictated through five areas of monopoly: technology, finance, control of natural resources, communications, and armaments.

The collapse of Fordism and of the welfare state in the West brings increasing chaos and a questioning of the European unification project, while the alternative plans for regionalization around the North American, European, and Japanese poles remain frail.[48]

In these circumstances the short term favors further implementation of the U.S. hegemonic plan, based essentially on military monopoly. This again checks the alternative of a rapprochement between Eastern Europe and Western Europe in what I have called "Eurasia unification," a nightmare prospect to Washington since 1945.[49] It also checks the only possible progressive alternative, the building of a polycentric world as the only means of creating the scope for autonomy needed to give the popular struggles room for achievement, though they may start small. I shall return in Chapter 5 to the new issues I broached in *Transforming the Revolution: Social Movements and the World System* (1990).

5

The Bourgeois National Project in the Third World: 1955-1990

When I was finishing my studies and returning to Egypt in 1957, two years after the Bandung Conference and one year after the nationalization of the Suez Canal, the vision under which we had lived in the postwar decade from 1945 to 1955 seemed to be being challenged. We had believed that a socialist revolution in unbroken stages was on the agenda throughout Asia and Africa. China, Vietnam, and the armed struggles in Southeast Asia provided the model. Communist parties everywhere were inspired by the model. There was no room for bourgeois leadership of national liberation. The bourgeoisie, in a comprador role everywhere, could only transmit a renewed imperialist domination under the aegis of the United States.

Suddenly—except for China, Vietnam, and North Korea—the emerging independent regimes in Asia settled down and the guerrillas vanished. Suddenly, the India of Nehru's Congress, Nasser's Egypt, and Sukarno's Indonesia took new initiatives on internal matters and in relations with imperialism on one side and the USSR and China on the other. These unexpected initiatives seemed to show that the bourgeoisie had not exhausted its historic role, and that the regimes were nothing if not bourgeois. The bourgeoisie claimed again to be national and guided the liberation under the new conditions which the exercise of power gave to it. It engaged in political and economic battles against imperialism through nationalization, including that of the Suez Canal. It refused to surrender to the orders of

U.S. military planners and rejected the Baghdad Pact (among others). It drew closer to the USSR and China. It undertook social reforms, especially land reforms. These facts could not be ignored.

From 1955 to 1990 debate focused on the central question: Was a national capitalist outcome possible in the third world? What could it really do and to what extent? Could it pave the way for a socialist replacement? This was not a bookish theoretical debate: the facts were there in the foreground. I personally plunged into the discussions throughout the period, in close connection with my professional work and my activist options. I shall have more to say on the personal link between my concerns as a socialist militant and the political atmosphere of the time.

This cycle is now over. I see the cycle as unfolding in two steps: deployment of the Bandung project from 1955 to 1975, followed by its stifling and dismantling, and the return of the third world to a comprador role from 1975 to 1990. The 1975 turning point seemed striking to me because of the nonaligned movement and the Group of 77 proposal for a New International Economic Order. Of course, internal evolution within the various third world countries did not necessarily run in strict parallel. There were delays; in some cases deployment or radicalization of the project came after 1975, and in others the stifling or turnaround came before that date.

The ebb and flow of the bourgeois national project in the third world was articulated in the general evolution of capitalism in the West, in international politics determined by the Cold War, and in the Sino-Soviet dispute.

I shall describe these main events as I see them today, with some indication of any gaps between the analysis I made at the time and what seems appropriate now. I shall anchor the analyses within the framework of my professional work and draw the theoretical lessons that seem appropriate today.

I put the evolution of China at the center of the debate, in part because of that country's intrinsic importance. From 1960 on, it offered a prospect of escape from the rut of Sovietism, which China claimed would lead to the restoration of capitalism. China drew significant conclusions about revolutionary strategies in the third world "storm zones" and about the international situation and strategies of imperialism versus "social imperialism."

Key dates in this period are as follows: 1957-1961: the Sino-Soviet dispute breaks out; 1966-1970: the Cultural Revolution occurs; 1969: military action in the border crisis at Ussuri reaches serious proportions. 1971: China is admitted to the United Nations and the United States begins to improve relations with China. 1976: the deaths of Zhou Enlai and Mao Zedong signal the exhaustion of the Maoist effort. 1984: the people's communes are abandoned. Since 1985: the Deng Xiaoping team in power chooses an opening to capitalism. I must admit that from 1957 to 1980 I was in almost total agreement with the analyses of the Communist Party of China, and from 1980 I have been critical of the capitalist overtures made there.

The Korean war (1950-1953) and the French phase of the Vietnam war (1945-1954) had already showed the limits to power of the Western imperialist bloc. The second phase of the Vietnam war (1965-1975) and the Cambodian war (1970-1975) showed that radicalization of national liberation was possible and was capable of defeating U.S. armies. The resonance in the third world of these victories should not be underestimated. It proved us right—we could do much better than the best of the bourgeois nationalist regimes. For us, as Egyptians and Arabs, there was an obvious comparison with our defeat by Israel in 1967. It was easy to understand the radicalization of the Palestinian movement, before and after Black September 1970, and to understand Che Guevara's slogan, "Create two, three, many Vietnams; that is the watchword." In Africa the collapse of

Portuguese colonialism in 1974 also showed the dividends that a protracted armed struggle could bring. However, the Algerian war (1954-1962) finished up in Boumedienne's radical nationalist regime, which seemed to us no more promising than Nasser's.

History did not stop at the Chinese Cultural Revolution or the victories in Vietnam and Cambodia in 1975. After these victories came an ebb, even in the most promising contexts. We gradually realized after 1975 what the historical limits of Maoism had been.[1] We were beginning to see that the battle was far from being won, and that even in China the forces of capitalism were going to have it their way.

North Korea patched up the wounds inflicted by the massive U.S. bombing and successfully cleared the hurdles of industrial and agricultural development. Yet its rigid political system did nothing to provide assurance about its future. In the very wake of its victory, Vietnam closed up in an even more disturbing pro-Soviet dogmatism. Nothing good was augured by Vietnam's Comecon membership in 1978, its vassalage of Laos and subsequent invasion of Cambodia in 1979, and the border war with China in 1979. The country's economic difficulties, stagnation, and incapacity to fully absorb the society of South Vietnam that had fought for liberation with its brothers and sisters in the north showed that radicalization could be caught in an impasse.

The ebb and flow of socialist forces in China, Korea, Vietnam, and Cambodia seemed to us to be caused by internal social conflicts and in no way by the external intervention factor. I have not changed my view on this: sufficiently advanced liberation diminishes the weight of the external factor, which is of course always unfavorable, and fully restores the decisive impact of the internal class struggle. But the external factor does not disappear. The total isolation of Cambodia in 1975, the real and imminent danger of famine in the capital, a Phnom Penh overpopulated because of the war—these factors broadly explained the regime's hard choices, which were subsequently to legitimize the Vietnamese invasion in some eyes. Vietnam's stagnation is undoubtedly explained by the dogmatism of its Communist party. Underlying this were the internal limitations of the country's socialist forces. But the tragic isolation imposed by the West was partly to blame. It is also true that the Hanoi leaders worsened their isolation by choosing to rely on the USSR rather than on China.

Alongside the ebb of socialist forces, Southeast Asia began its prodigious capitalist development, and this was quite unexpected by us (and by everyone, no matter what is said). The South Korean takeoff began with the overthrow of the U.S. puppet, President Syngman Rhee, and the military coup by General Park in 1961. Was the assassination of President Park in 1979 the beginning of the end of the "Korean miracle"? The first large-scale demonstrations broke out in 1980. I shall return to the significant but complex cases of South Korea and Taiwan. Contrary to the usual rule, the external factor played a positive role here. Together with Israel, South Korea and Taiwan received the bulk of U.S. aid throughout the postwar period. This aid made it possible to turn the corner of the difficult starting years in circumstances that cannot be matched elsewhere. In the face of a Communist "threat," the regimes in South Korea and Taiwan made reforms, especially around land distribution, that were unimaginable elsewhere, making hegemonic alliances, including with the rural bourgeoisie or large landholders (as in the north of India). The same "threat" enabled the regimes in South Korea and Taiwan to profit from their anticommunism: the United States accepted a nationalism they were fighting in other places. These countries were allowed to adopt a statist and protectionist strategy for industrialization contrary to the World Bank's insistence elsewhere.

Egypt, the Middle East, and Africa were my main concerns. Here too the Bandung project was deployed.

For Egypt the golden years of the project are the period from 1955 to 1967: the Suez Canal was nationalized in 1956, then foreign capital in 1957 and that of the Egyptian bourgeoisie in 1961, while the second land reform and the national charter made the socialist option official in 1961. It was not without weaknesses: the failure of the union with Syria (1958-1961); persistent anticommunism resulted in the dissolution of the Communist parties in 1965 and rejection of the best militants thereafter; stubborn refusal to democratize the system; tolerance for traditionalist Islamic discourse while banning progressive and lay, bourgeois, and socialist discourse; a drift into corruption. These factors led finally to the catastrophic defeat in the June 1967 war, when the U.S. and Israeli forces thought the moment opportune to strike a great blow.

Even before the regime reached the end of the road, by 1960 I thought, on the basis of three years' experience in the Nasser administration, that it had a poor chance of transcending its bourgeois limitations.[2] I strongly rejected the Moscow-inspired opportunist language of the so-called noncapitalist road.

I was delighted when after the 1967 defeat many young Egyptians with a socialist outlook went on the attack against the "new class." I admit I was disturbed to see that the regime, far from supporting the radicalization sought by these youth, preferred to make concessions to the *infitah* "open door" that emerged after Nasser's death in 1970 and the Sadat "coup" which broke with the left wing of Nasserism in May 1971. The open door to a comprador role that was under wraps until the 1973 war became an overt international and regional policy of alliance with the U.S. camp, the visit to Jerusalem in 1977 and the Camp David talks and treaty. The *infitah* did not seem to me a counterrevolution, as some Egyptian Communists less critical of

Nasserism believed, but rather a speedup of the normal evolution of the Nasserist system. Twenty years later I analyzed the open restoration of capitalism in the former USSR in the same way.

Whatever my own reservations, Nasserism was liberating and progressive in the eyes of the Arab peoples. My critical views were therefore continuously misunderstood and rejected during these twenty years.

The Ba'ath in the Mashreq was not a creation of Nasserism, but preceded it by several decades. Through mutual contact two brothers became enemies, wrecking the unity of Egypt and Syria, then the prospects for extension to Iraq in 1958. A historic opportunity of a rare kind was thrown away. I made a cool and calm analysis of the Nasserist experience in Egypt, the Ba'ath experience in Syria and Iraq, and the Boumedienne experience in Algeria. I concluded that even in the narrow sense, the systems were speedily stifled. Egypt was in crisis from 1965, and that is why the imperialists chose the moment to strike. The permanent crisis was latent in Syria. Ba'ath radicalism emerged after 1963 but was over before Hafez al-Assad assumed power in Damascus in 1971. He made a "realistic" choice of a disgraceful *infitah.* Iraq saw Abdel Karim Kassem accept the notion of a genuine popular alliance that included Communists and Kurds. But Abdel Salam Aref, with Nasser's sympathy, seized power in 1963 over Kassem's dead body, and the Ba'ath Party was responsible for a long train of criminal excesses. After 1968 the system hardened under the sway of General Hassan al-Bakr and, later, Saddam Hussein. Hussein's megalomania was encouraged by the West, and he embarked on a protracted war against Iran from 1980 to 1989. In spite of everything, Saddam's dictatorship did take the country into industrial, technological, and military modernization unparalleled in the modern Arab world. In 1990, the destruction of Iraq was decreed for this crime.

All these regimes seemed to me to share common basic features: a bourgeois vision of the future, deep anti-democracy and anticommunism, a mediocre pragmatic philosophy, overestimation of Soviet military support, and the cynical belief that they could play the American card if circumstances required.

The poor fringes of the Arab world and the Palestinian fight offered more hope. In 1964 the people of Khartoum overthrew the neocolonial dictatorship of General Ab-boud, in office since 1958, and imposed a genuinely democratic alliance. It was exceptional in the Arab world because it made room for Communists, trades unionists, and mass organizations. Sadly, our hopes in the new government were soon dashed. In the face of the gigantic problems created by Sudan's underdevelopment, what could be done in the short term to maintain and strengthen the vital mobilization of the people? In such conditions general elections, which should have brought a parliamentary majority of peasants, really brought in rural voters subjected to the pressures of their feudal Mahdist-Ansar masters. Corruption and inefficiency created the conditions for a return to dictatorship. This pattern recurred repeatedly in Sudan. Nimeiry came to power in 1969 with popular support, ridding himself in 1970 of Communists alleged in the next year to have fostered a coup attempt (and executing their leaders), and thenceforth relying on Islamic fundamentalism, Saudi Arabia, and the United States. Nimeiry was overthrown in 1985 by a democratic popular movement, hamstrung by the elections he had called. It was another opportunity for return to joint dictatorship by soldiers and Islamic fundamentalists. Through this long history the country has been in exhausting civil war, the non-Muslim south has lost its right to regional autonomy, and the country and society eventually disintegrated.

In North Yemen Egyptian military intervention from 1962 to 1965 followed the fall of the archaic regime of the imams. Did it save the country from a restoration sought by Saudi Arabia, or did it divert a potential radicalization of the people's struggle in the country and lead finally to an agreement dictated by Riyadh and Washington? I leaned toward the latter interpretation. I was encouraged from 1967 to 1968 by the radicalization of the South Yemen movement, which went on to institute the most authentic people's regime in the Arab world. The country has an obvious strategic position facing the Horn of Africa. Soviet influence, combined with internal weaknesses of the society and its vanguards—Maoist included—caused the system to collapse into meaningless internal struggles. It culminated in 1986 in the dubious Aden battles. Yemen unity, the choice of both regimes in 1989, is perhaps an honorable result in the circumstances and may safeguard the country's potential for further change.

The Palestinian people at last formed their own organization in 1964, distanced themselves from the Arab regimes, and gave birth to the Palestine Liberation Organization (PLO) under the chairmanship of Yasser Arafat. The radicalization was similar to that of numerous popular movements of the time and we expected much of it. Some Palestinian elements slid into terrorism and hijacking, although not the PLO as a whole, which is what Western and Zionist propaganda wanted the world to believe. Their behavior in the host countries of Jordan, and later Lebanon, facilitated a counterattack by local reactionary forces and imperialism. After the September 1970 massacres in Jordan, the Palestinians regrouped in Lebanon. Things remained much the same until the Palestinian people took the initiative in the struggle in the occupied territories. After 1988 the *intifada* changed the people's prospects.

Soon after Palestinian regrouping on Lebanese territory, Lebanon began a long series of civil wars, lasting from 1975 to the implementation of the Taief agreements after the second Gulf War (1990-1991). These wars, which I have written about several times, were primarily the result of Zionist aggression—with Western support—designed to break the country up: to create a Maronite, "pro-Western" mini-Lebanon and occupy the south—at the price of driving people out, as in Palestine—in order to control water resources deemed "vital" for Greater Israel. Israel's aggression in 1982 made achievement of this plan almost possible, but it was prevented by the Lebanese people's struggle and by Syria's subtle action, the latest reason for the hatred of Syria in the main Western media. Along with many Lebanese, I believed it essential to take a cold, hard look at the internal weaknesses of the Lebanese society, scarcely modernized by President Fuad Chehab's capitalism of the 1960s.

We did not expect miracles from the independence of Tunisia and Morocco in 1956. We all thought that the protracted Algerian war from 1954 to 1962 had created conditions for the radicalization of the people's movement in the country, and perhaps by example to the whole of North Africa. The Boumedienne experience from 1965 to 1978 brought an examination of the limits of the movement. I analyzed it as no more than a replica of Nasserism, although the financial prosperity brought by oil, especially after the 1973 price boom, delayed the day of reckoning. I was always puzzled by the enthusiasm of European third worldists and voiced my doubts about the Soviet-inspired technocratic theory of "industrializing industries." Conversely, I stressed the similarity between Algeria's evolution from left to right and the reverse evolution in Tunisia and Morocco.[3] The turn of events did not contradict my findings. The elimination of Ahmed Ben Salah in Tunisia in 1969, and the later slide to the right of the Benjedid Chadli regime in Algeria, did not seem to me counterrevolutions but merely crystallizations similar to Egypt's Sadatism. It was the usual instance of return to a comprador role. When the King of Morocco chose to annex the Western Sahara through the "green march" of 1975, and when Algeria took Mauritania to its bosom and tried to oppose Morocco, I was afraid that things would turn out as they did and put the struggle for the Maghreb and Arab unity in the wrong.

I could only sympathize with Muammar Gadafi's over-throw of the Libyan monarchy in 1969, though little could be expected from that country. I was not surprised by the "errors" of the new regime—supporting Nimeiry in 1971 and handing the Sudanese Communists over to him; by the excuses for the various "unions" with one or other partner, or his feeble interventions (such as the Tunisian comman-do Gafsa operation in 1980) and Chadian adventure, which was doomed to fail from the outset. This in no way excuses colonialist France for its intervention in Chad since 1968, well before Libya, or the United States for authorizing the criminal bombing of Tripoli in 1986. At the same time, I always looked sympathetically at the Libyan regime's greater efforts, especially for democratization and people's participation.

From my student days in France I had links with com-rades in the African movements. I passionately followed the uprising in Madagascar, the Mau Mau struggle in Kenya, and the UPC struggle in Cameroon. I was convinced that Africa was a whole, of which Egypt was a part. Imperialism forces us to struggle as one. I never accepted the specious racist prejudices that sub-Saharan Africa was too weak and must accept colonialism and neocolonialism, that the later EEC-ACP (African-Caribbean-Pacific) association was the best that could be done for the continent.

When I had to leave Egypt in 1960, I looked for a landfall. On September 20, 1960, during the congress of the RDA Sudanese Union, the Bamako regime opted for socialist radicalization. I had no hesitation in accepting a post I was offered in Mali.

In Cairo from 1958 to 1960 I had been following the preparations for African independence. I was not in France in 1958 when De Gaulle was recalled and came to power. I voiced my fears—later denied by the facts—of a right wing that would be more colonialist than the defunct Fourth Republic. I had not taken De Gaulle's last movement toward colonial "autonomy" seriously. I regarded Gaston Defferre's 1956 Loi-Cadre—enabling framework law—as a maneuver to balkanize Africa and to install biddable neocolonial regimes. At the Afro-Asian Peoples Solidarity Conference held in Cairo in 1957 in an atmosphere made tense by the Egyptian authorities' anticommunism, my own radical pan-Africanism was echoed in the statements by the comrades from Accra, capital of the first sub-Saharan state to be decolonized.

The years from 1960 to 1963 that I spent in Bamako saw the first wave of radicalization in Africa. Ghana's independence in 1957, Guinea's "no" vote to the Franco-African Community in the 1958 referendum, and Mali's decision in September 1960 to leave the community were the main signs of radicalization but not the only ones. Lumumbaism won the day in Congo Leopoldville. A similar radicalization could be expected from 1960 until 1963, when the central power in Leopoldville regained Kasai and Katanga provinces and concluded the wars of secession. In 1963 riots and demonstrations in Congo Brazzaville brought down the neocolonial regime of Fulbert Youlou.

These favorable evolutions were matched elsewhere by commonplace neocolonial regimes. In this tendentious atmosphere two blocs formed in 1961: the Casablanca bloc rallying the pan-African and socialist radicals behind Nasser's Egypt and Nkrumah's Ghana; and the Monrovia bloc rallying the neocolonial regimes. The latter were correctly believed to be frail, but unfortunately, the forces were not adequate to oust them in many countries. By contrast, the imperialist counteroffensive bore fruit. In Congo Leopoldville from 1963 the ominous Mobutu was lurking behind Kasavubu and became master of the field after 1965. He plunged his country into darkest night, where it remains to the present. He was supported despite all difficulties by the entire American and European West (I am thinking of French intervention at Kolwesi in 1978, in Shaba, the former Katanga, in 1982, and other occasions). When the two blocs decided in 1963 to merge in the Organization of African Unity, I thought this an acceptable compromise, although I had some doubts. Was the battle for radicalization already lost? I did not think so, and some later events were not to prove me wrong.

I did not share the childish optimism of those who saw in "African socialisms" a new and almost radiant path. The resemblance with Nasserism struck me. But no battle can be lost until it has been joined. Battle had to be joined. It was lost for all the familiar reasons: insufficient maturity of the avant garde; illusions about the Soviet "friend"; imperialist intervention; greed of the new embryonic, statist bourgeoisie. Nkrumah was overthrown in 1966 without understanding how he had contributed to sawing off the branch on which he sat. The same thing happened to Modibo Keita in 1968. The Guinea regime continued its wretched existence until the death of Sékou Touré in 1984. Its cornered dictatorship had long lost any progressive meaning for me and many others (though not for some). I published my analysis of these failures as early as 1965.[4]

The first wave in Africa was followed by a new radical upsurge. The Zanzibar Revolution in 1964 overthrew the sultan. Julius Nyerere opted for socialism in the Arusha Declaration of 1967. The corrupt neocolonial regime in Upper Volta received a first blow with Lieutenant-Colonel Sangoulé Lamizana's coup in 1966. But it was not until Thomas Sankara in 1983 that a new start was made when for the first time lessons were drawn from earlier failures and new, more popular and democratic working methods adopted. The mediocre neocolonialism in Somalia was ended by Siad Barre in 1969. The military in 1974 overthrew

Emperor Haile Selassie in Ethiopia, a country where the revolutionary forces seemed stronger than anywhere else in Africa. Yet the exceptionally brave Ethiopian revolutionaries were unable to avoid their country's total disintegration. They were divided into hostile factions, in the familiar fashion of Egypt, and paralyzed by a military dictatorship that was bogged down in the Eritrean war. That war was sustained in total ambiguity, sometimes by the imperialist powers and their clients in Saudi Arabia, Sudan, and Israel, and sometimes by the nationalist regimes in Syria and Iraq; it was backed to the hilt by the Soviet Union and Cuba. This was especially so during the Ogaden warfare in 1978 when Siad Barre acted the turncoat. The radical trend in Madagascar brought the fall of President Philibert Tsiranana in 1972, the radicalization promise in the fleeting government of Colonel Richard Ratsimandrava in 1975 that was consolidated from the moment when Captain Didier Ratsiraka took full command.

Other perhaps less promising changes indicated the incapacity of neocolonialism to overcome the constant crisis. Evidence of this crisis comes in the succession of coups in Congo and Dahomey, renamed Benin after Major Mathieu Kérékou's takeover in 1972, and Zambian President Kenneth Kaunda's slide toward statism in the 1970s. The crisis became more widespread in the late 1980s when democratic demands were made. Sometimes the demands were in a truly popular form, as in Mali where they ended Moussa Traoré's military dictatorship in 1992, and in the Ivory Coast and Kenya after the so highly praised economic "miracles" plunged into disaster. Sometimes the demands were in a mediocre form open to manipulation and control by the imperialist bosses. I include many of the "national conferences" for multiparty democracy under this heading.

The various responses to the crisis of neocolonialism cannot be classified simply. Despite the economic and social crisis deepening each year, there are examples of apparent continuity or political stability. Senegal may be the best example. Its comparative democracy and the skill of its political class makes it able to overcome the crises that recur without ever shattering the system. Nigeria is a similar example in its own way. The country holds fast without ever abandoning comprador neocolonialism (whatever the nationalist rhetoric of some regimes) and despite the diversity of its population, the interests combined in successive hegemonic blocs, and the threat of disintegration in the appalling Biafran War of 1967 to 1970. Nigeria goes through an endless round of military regimes and short-lived democracies. The oil resources have undoubtedly lubricated the wheels of this antiquated machine. Oil resources may broadly explain the stability of Gabon, and the low-key attitudes of the government and opposition in the Congo conflicts in 1992 with an honorable outcome in President Pascal Lissouba's election victory and the possible revival of the Congolese Labor Party.

How do we judge the return of Nkrumahism to Ghana from 1979 brought by the successive coups by Jerry Rawlings but eroded by the notorious "structural adjustment" policies strengthening the local comprador bourgeoisie and marginalizing the existing popular organizations? How do we judge the regime emerging from the popular movement in Uganda that succeeded Idi Amin, driven out in 1979, and the pathetic figure of Milton Obote? The Ugandan regime was also paralyzed by the sacrosanct "structural adjustment."

The crisis of neocolonialism may also end in the total disintegration of society. Liberia, Chad, and Somalia are veritable instances.

The protracted war of liberation in the Portuguese colonies led naturally to radicalization of the movement, at least at the level of its ideological positions. I personally had some doubts about the theory advanced by Amilcar Cabral that "the revolutionary petite bourgeoisie must be capable of committing suicide as a class."[5] The abrupt collapse of the Portuguese system in 1974 unexpectedly hastened the coming of independence and strongly reduced the chances of this suicide.

In Angola the National Front for the Liberation of Angola (FNLA) and National Union for the Total Independence of Angola (UNITA) did not have the standing they claimed but the People's Movement for the Liberation of Angola (MPLA) could not claim to be the sole liberation force. UNITA, supported to the hilt by the Western powers and South Africa, waged war for more than seventeen years until the South African forces were roundly beaten at Cuito Cuanavale by joint Cuban and MPLA troops. South Africa was obliged in 1988 to accept the Protocol of Geneva, whereby elections were to be held in Namibia after the staged withdrawal from Angola of Cuban troops and South African forces. The disastrous effects of the war cost the MPLA opportunities it might have had—if it had kept aloof from its Soviet protector and avoided foundering in dogmatic rhetoric—to become a genuinely radical popular force. Angola with its oil revenue does not differ much from the corrupt institutions of the neocolonial powers to be found elsewhere in Africa. Circumstances are ripe for an eventual power sharing with UNITA, if the United States wants this solution and desists from imposing Savimbi as the regional substitute for a threadbare Mobutu.

Similar effects eventually followed in Mozambique from the war which the Mozambique National Resistance (Renamo), supported like UNITA by South Africa and its Western masters, imposed on the Mozambique Liberation Front (Frelimo). Despite the concessions in the Nkomati Agreement of 1984, Frelimo ceased to operate as a unifying force in society; Renamo was never more than armed bandits, even when it shared posts with its opponent. The danger of Somali-style disintegration was real. I do not believe that Western politicians were unaware of this. As in Afghanistan, they pursued worst-case policies in order to destroy the potential radicalization of the people at the cost of the total destruction of the society.

The African Independence Party of Cape Verde (PAICV) was defeated in elections in 1991. This was a reminder that despite remarkable achievements in a country seemed doomed to stagnate, the party had underestimated its own shortcomings in democratic administration and the particular character of a country closer to the West Indies than to the African mainland.

The hard kernel of colonization in Africa was South Africa, to which the Rhodesian whites believed they could hitch their wagon by the unilateral declaration of independence in 1965, with support from Britain, the mother country, playing out a farce with customary hypocrisy. In 1980 the liberation struggle secured the independence of Zimbabwe. At what price? The Patriotic Front, mainly the Zimbabwe African National Union (ZANU), agreed at the Lancaster House conference in London to a constitution blocking any serious attempt at social or land reform. The Front embarked on a schizophrenic course: an undoubtedly well-meant leftist discourse accompanied by structural adjustment policies that brought an endless worsening of the social crisis.

Is the same solution in prospect for South Africa? In my analysis of the specific character of the country I stressed aspects too often neglected.

The first aspect was the certain failure of the white power plan to make "their" country a modern industrial power and reduce black workers to near slavery. The project begun with British settlement a century ago has taken clear shape under the apartheid regime of the past four decades. But South African industry was not competitive with that of Latin America and Asia and was, according to the principle criterion of capitalist globalization, of no more worth than that of other "industrialized" African and Middle East countries (Egypt, Iraq, Algeria). Pretoria's unconditional Western backers always omitted to say this—undoubtedly because of racism. In fact, South Africa was doomed to certain failure because of the resistance of the black working class from Sharpeville in 1960 to Soweto in 1976, followed by the widespread ungovernability that led President F. W. de Klerk to accept negotiation after 1990. The failure was also due to the incredible waste involved in maintaining a white minority with Western consumption patterns but without Western productivity.

The second aspect was that South Africa concentrated in its territory a kind of microcosm of the world capitalist system: a minority of first world consumers, a significant active reserve army of labor concentrated in the mines and settlement agriculture and populating the townships, and a no less sizable reserve relegated to the peasant life on the reserves and bantustans or the informal sectors around the towns.

What was to be expected of the negotiation process? Was it another Lancaster House taking the form of a federal constitution to protect the advantages of the white minority from the project's historic failure? Internal and external U.S. and European pressures went that way and trumpeted the advantage the black majority would inherit with the wonderful industrial base. In the spirit of our age, the majority was asked merely to help the country become competitive. In other words, the worker majority was asked to go on paying for what capital had failed to do, even with worldwide financial, economic, and political support and despite atrocious methods. I was not always sure that the majority forces in the South African liberation camp were aware that they might be offered a fatal trap. To follow that road might imply in turn maintenance or worsening of the gap between the industrial townships and the bantustans or informal sector. It was clear that de Klerk and his Western masters were counting on this scenario to weaken the position of the African National Congress (ANC) and its allies.

The Bandung project was implemented in Asia in a more striking way and could boast of less tender achievements. The prevailing view in the third world of the Congress Party of India is highly favorable; it points to parliamentary democracy, competitive industry, green revolution, technological progress, even military success (India had the atom bomb from 1974). The Indian left has correctly hedged these hasty judgments. The Indian industrial bourgeoisie, allied with the large landholders in the north of the country and the state technocracy, has never envisaged conflict with transnational capital, even before Nehru's death in 1964. It is paying a price, and India's technological and financial control is more apparent than real. Parliamentary democracy is the only reasonable way of managing the various hegemonic social alliances from one region to another of the subcontinent. It does not avoid political marginalization of the popular classes; on the contrary, it depends upon it. Indian neutralism is no real nuisance to U.S. hegemony, despite India's closeness to China in the 1950s. The border conflicts of 1959 and 1962 were at bottom exploited by the Indian ruling class. The stifling of the plan that was nationalist in the beginning has become evident. This stifling brought on the state of emergency in 1975. It allowed the right-wing government under Morarji Desai to pursue a policy more open to Western interests from 1977 to 1979. It exacerbated ethnic clashes, with Sikh concerns leading to the assassination of Indira Gandhi in 1984. Subsequent governments look set on a comprador role.

Pakistan has never really emerged from a comprador role; as in Saudi Arabia, this is indicated by a natural alliance between dictatorship (military in Pakistan) and Islamic fundamentalist discourse. Zulfiqar Ali Bhutto's brief attempt to break with tradition was overthrown in the coup d'état by General Zia ul Haq in 1977. His daughter Benazir Bhutto's attempt a decade later also failed. It is a state that refused to admit what it is: Muslim India. It was obliged to mobilize to fight India for Kashmir, in 1965-1966 and in 1971, when an independent Bangladesh emerged. Pakistan earns its keep through the services it gives the United States, including intervention in Afghanistan in the 1980s.

The Western left hailed with enthusiasm Sri Lanka's attempt to combine its bourgeois national development project with a social policy better than elsewhere. The left did not see that the two aims were in total contradiction. The predictable failure of the attempt has led to horrifying guerrilla violence that has continued since 1983.

President Ahmed Sukarno's Indonesia was one of the pillars of the Bandung project in Southeast Asia. This explains the hatred the Western powers had for him. He was ousted in 1967 in a CIA-inspired coup d'état. Hundreds of thousands of Communists were massacred, thus ending the "danger" of a popular radicalism that might have gone beyond Sukarno's policy. There is no "miracle" in sight to match the country's surrender, anymore than there is in the Philippines, where local reactionary forces—supported by Washington, of course—justified the bloody dictatorship of President Ferdinand Marcos until 1986 by the constant civil war forced by peasant revolt. The urban uprising that brought Corazón Aquino to power in 1986 was unable to unify its forces with those of the endemic rural rebellion and end the neocomprador role behind a democratic facade on which the United States relied.

Thailand played on its strategic position near Vietnam and achieved more. It is now included in the semi-industrialized part of the new third world, although ranking below Korea and Taiwan. Malaysia emulates its southern neighbor under the aegis of overseas Chinese capital in association with the state.

U.S. military strategy for the region, long obsessed with China and Vietnam, led to the imposition in 1967 of the Association of South-East Asian Nations (ASEAN). The organization may change character to become a pole of comparatively autonomous regional forces, while remaining an instrument of concern to local ruling classes.

Turkey became an unconditional ally of the United States in western Asia because of its fear of the USSR. Washington never failed to use its presence to erase Kemalism, the forebear of Nasserism and the Bandung project. Kemalism had a come-back twice: first in 1961, after General Cemal Gursel ended the comprador regime of Prime Minister Adnan Menderes, and then in 1980, with a new military regime. Kemalism had been long worn-out and was never able to surpass itself or give way to a popular, democratic movement with the potential to do so. This may explain its slide into chauvinism in 1983 with the Turkish Republic of Northern Cypus. Turkey was obsessed with its application to join the EEC, refused in Brussels in 1989, and developed an industrial competitiveness that put it in the front rank of the new third world. One wonders if the collapse of the USSR and the new Middle East situation will encourage Turkey to expand by turning its back on Europe. This could revive a "neo-Ottomanism."

The dictatorship of the Shah of Iran, restored after the fall of Prime Minister Mohammed Mossadegh in 1953, put the country on a modernizing statist path. It had a conservative social policy which did not contradict world capitalism but did quite well. The conservative and overtly anti-democratic style and the unreservedly Western cultural option provided was its Achilles' heel. The Islamic fundamentalist revolution from 1978 to 1979 ended the experiment of that Bandung from the right but could offer no genuine alternative that went beyond religious rhetoric. The new team of President Ali Akbar Hashemi Rafsanjani opted naturally for a formula like that of Saudi Arabia and

Pakistan. It combined a return to a cheap comprador role (giving Iran less status than it had under the Shah) and religious discourse as extreme as it is formalistic.

If Iran is no more a threat to capitalist domination, could Afghanistan ever have become one? A minor revolution in 1978 ended the regime of Lieutenant-General Daud Khan and introduced a modernizing populist team that would have found its own limits. The paracommunist ideology through which the modernizing intellectuals expressed themselves would, I think, have been gradually adjusted. Soviet intervention from 1979, jockeying one section of the intelligentsia against another, gave the United States an unexpected opportunity to bog down Soviet armies in the region and forestall the Afghan modernizers. The Western powers supported the "Islamic fundamentalists." After their "victory" in 1992 the fundamentalists plunged the country into constant war more frightful than the one before. The Western powers once again showed the cynicism with which they regard the peoples of the region and their own lipservice to democracy. The attempt by Dr. Najibullah Ahmadzai to organize resistance after 1986, when the Soviet "ally" became a turncoat, was too late to prevent the worst.

Latin America was not represented at Bandung and not expected to join the nonaligned movement for at least three reasons. Latin America is made up of states that have been independent since the nineteenth century. It is dominated by European culture. The perennial U.S. influence was accepted by the ruling classes. However, in the period after World War II Latin America has followed a parallel evolution to that in Asia and Africa under the Bandung banner. The basic reason is obvious: Latin America's peripheral capitalism places it in a similar objective situation in the world system. Three cases should be included among radical third world experiences.

Cuba freed itself from the yoke of Washington's lackeys by chasing Batista out of Havana in 1959. The United States was not slow to see a real danger in Castroism, as is evidenced in the early and unsuccessful attempt to win the country back in 1961 in the Bay of Pigs invasion. The Washington threat lay heavy on Cuba, which was under an economic boycott by the United States and its European allies, increasing its dependence on the USSR. In the Soviet nuclear missile crisis of 1962 Cuba was probably saved from invasion by the diplomatic footwork of Nikita Khrushchev and Fidel Castro. But this further contributed to Cuba's adherence to the Soviet model, decreasing its potential for more democratic and less artificial evolution.

Under Salvador Allende from 1970 to 1973, Chile was a democracy in the conventional parliamentary sense of the term. Chilean democracy succumbed to blows organized by Washington. The bloody dictatorship of General Augusto Pinochet, with support from the United States and Europe, pursued a comprador role. Is Chile the success it is now said to be beyond the corridors of the World Bank? Is it a model for the neocapitalists in Warsaw and Moscow? Not in my view, and not only because of the exorbitant social cost of structural "adjustment." In worldwide capitalism, Chile remains a subordinate producer, unable to go beyond export production work for the benefit of dominant capital and its local allies, and hence unable to offer its people the prospect of an agreeable future.

In Nicaragua, the Sandinista National Liberation Front ousted the Somoza regime in 1979. The Sandinista movement had learned from history and tried to avoid confusing excessive statism with socialism; it tried to practice genuine democracy and to maintain diverse external relations. This did not escape U.S. hostility, which financed and supported the contras in their fight against the Managua administration. Europe was feebly dragged behind Washington. Sandinista withdrawal from government after the 1990 elections was an honorable outcome, leaving the popular elements to fight another day.

For Latin America as a whole, the 1960s and 1970s meant semi-fascist military dictatorships supported by the ironically named Alliance for Progress established in 1961 by President John Kennedy, a Democrat. The dictatorships claiming legitimacy as modernizers were to contradict the thesis of *desarrollismo* in the 1960s—that modernization should be the basis of democratization of society. The thesis failed to see that modernization within globalized capitalism disadvantaged the ordinary people to the benefit of the middle classes, the mainstay of the autocratic regimes. Hence the economic "miracles" the World Bank hailed at the time provided right-wing versions of a bourgeois nationalist model, whereas Bandung offered the left-wing populist model. Brazil was a prime example of the former. President João Goulart was overthrown in 1964; Brazil was under a dictatorship until the 1985 elections.

The two models had more in common than is often thought. Similar goals were pursued in Argentina, against a Peronist populist background, by Lieutenant-General Jorge Videla's military junta, which took power in 1976. After the junta was ousted, a nationalist trend developed in 1982 with the war over the Malvinas Islands (Falklands); the trend persists to this day. The bloodless coup in Peru in 1968 came close to the Bandung populist model. Because the model was blocked, social upheaval followed and the Shining Path (*Sendero Luminoso*) movement emerged.

The 1980s meant widespread crisis for the semi-fascist and the populist bourgeois national projects, which were caught in a stranglehold of foreign debt. The Mexico moratorium in 1982 marked the outbreak of the financial crisis. The United States then discovered a "democratic" mission to control the crisis by methods that eased the burden on the working people and the middle classes. The vulnerability of the restricted democracies in place indicated the historic limitations of a comprador role. For example, in Argentina Dr. Raúl Alfonsín, who was eagerly elected in 1983, gave way to the wishy-washy Carlos Menem in the 1989 presidential elections.

In the West Indies social structures inherited from a different colonial history brought reactions to the new challenges similar to those of Asia and Africa. We saw in Jamaica a Bandung populism during the first premiership of Michael Manley from 1972 to 1980. A similar approach in Grenada was nipped in the bud by the U.S. invasion in 1983. A people's movement brought election victory in Haiti in 1990 for Father Jean-Bertrand Aristide. It was a short-lived victory: the military coup d'état came as a reminder that Westerners do not practice democracy except when it serves their interests.

The 1955-1975 period was the period of development ideology. The Bandung regimes, whether left-wing populist or right-wing conservative, realized that their bourgeois national project required fresh energy in "adjustment" by the North to make the demands of globalized capitalist expansion more tolerable. The proposed reform of the New International Economic Order came under this heading. It was rejected by the West, as a reminder that a bourgeois national construct on the periphery of the system was utopian. What followed was unilateral adjustment of the peripheries to the demands of global capital domination—in other words, a return to the comprador role.

Certain key dates and events stand out in the Bandung project and in the common front of the nonaligned nations and the Group of 77 (with the latter coupling Latin America to Asia and Africa). The Organization of Petroleum Exporting Countries (OPEC) was established in 1961 but went unnoticed until 1973, when economic and political events enabled it to win its first great victory. There was a series of summit conferences of the nonaligned movement, beginning with the Belgrade summit of 1961 and continuing to the recent summit meeting in Indonesia in 1992. The Group of 77 has consistently made constructive proposals to the United Nations Conference on Trade and Development (UNCTAD) and these have just as consistently been rejected by the Western countries in the OECD.

To center the period's history on the implementation of the bourgeois national project in the peripheries may seem outlandish to some. I stand firm on my opinion: throughout the postwar period the world order revolved around the huge political and social changes that totally transformed the societies of Africa, Asia, and Latin America and thereby of the world as a whole. These three continents, which housed the majority of the world's population, underwent major qualitative changes with long-term impacts, while comparatively modest changes took place in the societies of central capitalism.

In some ways the changes in capitalism in the dominant centers played a decisive role in the evolution of the world system. I noted the information technology revolution; the consequent globalization of communications, media, and culture; nuclear weapons and missiles; the breadth of ecological damage on a global scale. I thought it relevant to center the changes around the two main axes.

The Fordist model was wearing out. It was associated with the effective dissociation between the scope for reproduction of world capital and the scope for political and social management of the conditions of that reproduction, which remained fragmented and distributed among national states. The dissociation eroded the effectiveness of the national policies on which the social-democratic welfare state was built. In Europe it is the great challenge of the twenty-first century.

The imbalance between the United States and the other centers of world capitalism, Europe and Japan, was reduced so quickly that it seemed to indicate an American decline. Did this mean that the European construct, originally conceived as a subsystem of overtly unbounded and globalized capitalism, was to become a competing center to the United States and Japan? I voiced my doubts. I observed that Europe and Japan remained aligned behind the United States, playing down their mercantile conflicts, and that the Western bloc had never shown the slightest crack in the face of the South (and the recent and contemporary East). De Gaulle had hopes of Europe and the Soviet Union drawing closer together and withdrew French forces from the NATO command in 1986. Soviet strategy sought and failed to break up the Atlantic bloc, with the policy of the carrot from Khrushchev and Gorbachev, and the stick from Brezhnev.

The crisis began after 1970 and is the background for the U.S. abandonment of the gold standard in 1971. Productive investment collapsed and has never recovered. Gigantic growth in U.S. military expenditure and financial speculation filled the vacuum created by the collapse, but the solidarity of the centers has remained intact despite everything. The dollar has fluctuated enormously: less than 4 French francs (FF) in 1978, over 10 FF in 1985, and back to less than 5 FF in 1992. The interpenetrating of capitals through the centers makes the previously effective national solutions obsolete.

A solution to this structural crisis of capitalism requires the recomposition in the West of new socialist forces operating on a European continental scale, and replacing the failing national state with a supranational state capable of handling the new social compromise at this scale.

This seemed to be on the horizon in the 1970s after the great ideological shake-up of 1968. Willy Brandt became chancellor of the Federal Republic of Germany in 1969. The Labour Party returned to office in Britain in 1970. Fascism had collapsed in Portugal and Spain by 1975. By 1980 Greece was free of the military dictatorship in place since 1967. François Mitterand was elected president of France in 1981. But all the hopes we had of the period went up in smoke, because the Western left missed the opportunity of a revival. When the Eastern Europe and former-USSR systems collapsed between 1989 and 1992, nothing was in place to start a global reconstruction of Europe on the basis of progressive social compromises. Quite the reverse, as the dominant right saw an opportunity to turn Eastern Europe into "their" Latin America. A unified Germany, with a dominant position in this new prospect of capitalist polarization, distanced itself from the European plan that had given it a platform, and put out of joint the new step the project was supposed to take in the Maastricht Treaty of 1992.

Without a counterweight from the left, chaos automatically followed the short-term view taken by capital. The European continent was affected, as was evident in Yugoslavia. It was also an opportunity for the United States to resume the offensive as a global policeman (the Gulf War showed this in 1991) and demonstrate that world management through the market was utopian. Such management required powerful military intervention. This was to be more and more feared as the disastrous social effects of U.S. management led to uncontrollable outbursts.

The wearing out of the socialist Soviet alternative and its subsequent collapse was the third aspect of the postwar period. From the CPSU's Twentieth Congress in 1956, the system inherited from the Stalin era tried to reform itself. It could not succeed. I maintained that the critique of the system had been made from the right—from Khrushchev to Gorbachev. It reflected the bourgeois aspirations of the ruling class. The final collapse was more of a speed-up in the direction the system was traveling than a counter-revolution. It began in the late 1960s after the invasion of Czechoslovakia in 1968. The Polish uprising came after Wladyslaw Gomulka was replaced in 1970 by Edward Gierek. The failure was already complete by 1985 when Gorbachev embarked on perestroika, which led to the collapse. I was always critical of reform proposals; hence my association with the journal *Révolution* from 1963 and my Maoist stand.[6]

The USSR escaped from isolation after 1955 by spotting a trump card in a strategic alliance with the liberation movements and third world countries in conflict with imperialism. The alliance was positive, whatever my view of the character of the Soviet system. It obliged the imperialists to reduce the violence of their interventions. The Gulf War and the terrorist methods of destruction of an entire country employed immediately after the USSR disappeared from the scene are sad indications of the natural violence with which imperialism acts when it is not constrained to moderation.

Soviet intervention in the third world also had a serious negative side. It was not because the USSR tried at any time to expand socialism and reduced its distant allies to vassals. It was because the USSR always sought to legitimize its intervention in an ideological discourse consistent with its internal discourse of "socialism." Alliance with the national bourgeoisies was not presented as such but as support to "progressive forces" in "transition to socialism." The muddled theories of the "noncapitalist road" were devised for the purpose. These terms were taken up by the radical left in national liberation movements and even by the leading Marxist circles. This only worsened the confusion and left working people unprepared to react appropriately to the erosion and collapse of the Bandung project.

In these circumstances a serious and scientific analysis was demanded of the character and objectives of USSR international policy. Was it a defensive strategy whose apparent offensive was merely an exercise of pressure on the Western powers? I supported this view and suggested that the USSR's strategic aim was to break the Atlantic bloc, not to treat Europe like Finland, but to broaden the scope for the contradiction between the United States and Europe, or even to create conditions to move closer to

Europe in a common capitalist framework that would for the USSR be neocapitalist. I did not rule out lapses into social imperialism, as in Afghanistan.

The postwar cycle is definitely closed. The collapse of the Bandung project has surely proved us right in retrospect. Were we wrong in the years from 1945 to 1955 to believe that the national bourgeoisie had finished its historic role? Were we wrong to believe that the project for national capitalist development on the periphery was obsolete and utopian? Surely it was hasty to accuse of "ultraleftism" those who stressed the impasse of the Bandung project, its bourgeois character, the opportunism of the spurious concept of the "noncapitalist road."

I do not suggest that my analyses of events, often produced in the middle of the struggle, were always necessarily correct and sufficient—or seem so today. I read again what I wrote at the time and have recalled in the preceding pages. I remain convinced that in their general line the analyses were correct. I should go so far as to say that they were sometimes highly perceptive, although such a statement may seem lacking in modesty. I can give some examples.

It was almost prophetic in 1960 to predict the "natural" end of Nasserism in its *infitah* open-door forms. I warned against an overall neocomprador solution in the Middle East, where Israel was to be included in the region (even though only a few years ago this was not understood by close friends in Cairo). I analyzed the the Ivory Coast "miracle" after 1965, which contrasts with the World Bank's prognosis, itself contradicted by events. I supported the position in 1975 that in Angola the determined search for a coalition government of the liberation movements was the best solution. I do not know if this search would necessarily have been successful, but I do not believe everything necessary was done to try it. Today, after some seventeen years of useless war, the solution may be imposed but in farcical form! I voiced fears from 1972 to 1974 about Zimbabwe and South Africa—that a compromise would be possible in the region, as it was to be in the Lancaster House conference for Zimbabwe in 1980 and as a "federal solution" in the South African negotiation process.

I have never been a better prophet than anyone else. I did not try to be, and I stressed that the future always remained open. It seemed to me that on principle one always has to act so that the best evolution should have the best chance, and that the worst should be avoided—even if it sometimes seemed the most natural. This approach has often brought me bitter and malicious criticism as "bourgeois opportunism" from genuine leftists (who have often moved on to anti-Marxism).

I attempted gradually to deepen the analysis, moving from actual events to the internal logic of capitalism and a Marxist understanding of them. I see now that I went through various steps, which I shall summarize here. In the years from 1960 to 1975 I entirely shared the Maoist view of these problems and nothing more, meaning I did not see the historic limitations of Maoism. I remained within the framework of the problematic of "bourgeois revolution or socialist revolution" (through an uninterrupted revolutionary process). I rejected the first path (even in the concealed form of the "noncapitalist road") and believed the second to be objectively possible. In the same framework I regarded Sovietism as a deviation from a revolution whose goal of building socialism would obviously be difficult but was realistic. Then from 1980 to 1985 I began to challenge this problematic. As I deepened the analysis of polarization, I began to believe that the true challenge was posed in other terms, the immediate or almost immediate building of socialism and national capitalist development being alternative utopias, both stemming from an inadequate analysis of polarization.

I propose now to consider in these terms the challenge we face for the future.

Restoration of the periphery to a comprador role is an accomplished fact. World Bank structural adjustment policy is its manifestation. But restoration to a comprador role does not end history. Bandung had many forms. According to circumstances and social and political conditions peculiar to each country and the play of world and regional forces, we have several families of transformations that have gradually occurred in the postwar cycle.

(1). Above-board capitalist development accompanied by a so-called liberal ideology, although often characterized by state intervention, determinedly modernist and open to the world system (but seeking to control that opening). South Korea, Taiwan, Mexico, Brazil, Turkey, Iran under the Shah, and some other Asian countries are typical of this model.

(2). Populist, strongly statist, and never democratic experiences, ambivalent about integration into globalization (with stronger emphasis on control of external relations than the preceding countries, or purporting to want this), usually self-styled as socialist and often supported by the USSR. Some of these experiences have gone further in industrialization, and others less so according to their historical legacy. Nasser's Egypt, Algeria, and Iraq are examples of the first kind, and Tanzania and Ghana of the second.

(3). Experiences regarded as "Marxist," as in China, North Korea, and Cuba. They begin, as in the Soviet experience, from a radical revolution inspired by the doctrine of the Third International. They are now aiming, in China openly, for a capitalism that purports to control its relations with the dominant world system.

(4). Experiences that have never escaped from a commonplace neocolonial framework, recording growth in some cases (the Ivory Coast and Kenya) or obstinate stagnation in others (the Sahel countries) in totally passive surrender to external stimulus.

There are many crosses between these theoretical families and sometimes a shift from one strategy to the other in the political phases of modern history. India, for example, is a mixture of groups 1 and 2, while whole regions of the subcontinent remain a fourth world country. South Africa would have been classified in group 2 by a humorist who forgot that Afrikaner state populism was of the racist minority. It operated as if it were in group 1, but failed to realize capitalist goals. Vietnam is formally in group 3 but remains a fourth world country.

These huge transformations have bequeathed us a different situation from that of 1945. Here one must take as key to the analysis the criterion of globalized capitalism, in the presence or absence of segments of the local productive system "competitive" on a world scale or capable of becoming so without too much trouble. We have therefore distinct third and fourth worlds.

The new third world is made up of all the countries in groups 1, 2, and 3 that have achieved sufficient modernization according to the criterion of world competition. In this group come all the big countries of Latin America, East Asia (China, both Koreas, Taiwan), Eastern Europe, and the former USSR. This, I believe, is tomorrow's real periphery. It is obvious that their peoples may not necessarily accept the cruel fate capital has reserved for them.

The new fourth world is made up of all the other countries in Africa and the Arab and Islamic world. They come in a variety of shapes and sizes. Some have taken steps to industrialization but have failed to become competitive (Egypt, Algeria, and South Africa, for example). Others have not embarked on an industrial revolution (sub-Saharan Africa, the West Indies, Central America, Pakistan, Bangladesh, and Indonesia). Some are financially "rich," like the thinly populated oil producers (the Gulf states and Gabon). Others are to varying degrees "poor" (from the Ivory Coast to Somalia). My criterion is not per capita income but the capacity for productive integration in the world system.

Some countries are a mixture of these characteristics. India is a classic example. Some are trickier to classify as they are potentially or partially capable of moving from fourth to third world status: Zimbabwe, South Africa, Egypt, Algeria, or Vietnam, for example.

These third and fourth world peoples all face the same challenge, but the circumstances of their fight are different. The challenge comes from peripheral capitalism that has nothing good to offer in social or political terms to the ordinary majority. As I said in Chapter 1, the third world peripheral social formations juxtapose a significant active army of labor and a reserve army that cannot be absorbed. This creates objective conditions for a strong popular social alliance capable of crystallizing through struggles over management of the productive system and democratiza- tion of politics and society. The barriers to this crystallizing are also real and diverse. The ideological obstacle in the legacy of Sovietism or the historical limitations of Maoism are not the least part of it. Will the peoples manage to free themselves from the illusions of capitalism and avoid foundering in jingoistic nationalism? China is also in this group. Can its avant-garde revive Maoism with a genuinely democratic component—autonomous organization of the ordinary people to counter concessions made to capitalism?

In the fourth world social formations we are facing a situation in which the concept of "people" remains ill- defined in the absence of a viable productive system. These "peoples" are in conflict with power sytems which are themselves not rooted in a solid productive system. These social formations may look "rich" or "poor." They may be nonindustrialized or so badly industrialized that the policy of return to a comprador role puts local industry at risk of being dismantled. I have explained how a disastrous but real aspect of the problem was a slide into conflict in imaginary realms. In the Middle East and Muslim Arab world this factor is currently the main obstacle to crystallization of a democratic and popular alternative. The best guarantee for success in the imperialist agenda to restore the region to a comprador role is the alliance of oil wealth and the obsolete traditionalist discourse of Islam, notwithstanding its "fundamentalist" aspirations. It is obviously under way. Anti-democratic handling of social conflicts becomes necessary because the agenda offers nothing to ordinary people and can be implemented under cover of religious traditionalism. In sub-Saharan Africa, the flight into myth may take other forms, such as ethnicity, and can lead to a country's total disintegration, as happened in Ethiopia, to the detriment of the future. The weaknesses of society find an echo likewise in the ambiguities of "battles for democracy." Without a crystallization of popular social forces capable of endowing democracy with a progressive content, what can be expected of multiparty politics and elections?

As soon as my doctoral thesis was accepted I returned to Egypt, and in January 1958 I took up a post in the Economic Development Organization, known in Arabic as Mouassassa. The institution had been established in the wake of the 1957 nationalizations and was to manage the substantial state sector in industry, trade, banking, insurance, and transport. The director and my immediate boss was a friend and comrade, Ismail Sabri Abdallah. Isabelle became a local employee of the French *lycée* at Ma'adi. My parents lived in our family home at Port Said.

At the Mouassassa I dealt with a variety of matters, and as I was in the research department, I decided to take a close look at each of the broad sectors in the modern Egyptian economy—cotton and textiles, steel and engineering, banking and insurance, transport, etc.—and to examine their history, problems, and development prospects. I left behind a mass of files that might be useful to students interested in the country's past and the Nasser period. I also examined the papers on the High Dam. Without this giant project, Egypt with its 50 million inhabitants would have been unable to cope as it did with the drought that struck Africa in the later years. When the dam was opened and new land was recovered from the sand, a shortage of resources meant it was insufficiently drained. I can state here that many of the excellent Egyptian technicians who prepared the project were fully cognizant of many of the problems. The World Bank was sympathetic to the project but thought it could impose purely political conditions on Egypt—no Czech weapons! The World Bank refused finance. Soviet-aided construction was much cheaper than the Bank's earlier plan forecast. The Americans were resentful that the Bank's refusal had no effect and made a critique of the project, which was too readily taken up by ecologists but overlooked that water in Egypt is the essential element for life.

My duties kept me in close touch with the manner in which the new public sector was managed, and with the discussions and decisions among company boards. I learned much. I saw how the "new class" was being shaped, how the private interests of many of these gentlemen (there were few women involved) determined too many decisions. I saw how the workers' representatives, a Nasserist innovation excellent on paper, were marginalized and tricked or bought off.

I did not spend all my time within the walls of the Mouassassa. When I left the office I was a militant like others, and my active sympathy was with the Egyptian Communist Party, as I said above. I was more aware than when I was a student in France that two opposing lines were emerging and had always been present in the Egyptian movements. I followed closely the Sino-Soviet dispute when it ceased to be secret and made the natural connection between the leftist line that seemed to me correct and the emerging criticism of Moscow from Maoism. I was always in a minority with others such as Fawzy Mansour.

We had a hard time in 1958 and 1959. The honeymoon between the regime and the Communists after the Suez nationalization in 1956 was short-lived. Communist criticism of the anti-democratic and bureaucratic approach to the merger of Egypt and Syria was not accepted. On January 1, 1959, the police arrested thousands of Communists. I escaped the first round of arrests but knew the net was closing in. In January 1960 I left Egypt.

I wrote *L'Egypte nassérienne* in 1960, but no publisher would touch it until after 1963: Nasser was supporting the liberation struggle in Algeria and must not be upset.

During the nine months I spent in Paris from January to September 1960 I was working in the research and finance section of the Finance Ministry, headed at the time by a remarkable intellectual, Claude Gruson, to whom I had been introduced by a good friend, Charles Prou. I learned much there. I sometimes played with economic models, such as the famous variable price financial model the mathematician Nataf and I devised. I had no intention of staying in France or anywhere else in the West. I always believed my place was in the African and Arab third world.

An opportunity arose in Mali where my friend Jean Bénard was a roving adviser on economic matters. I was glad to take the offer. In Bamako I found people I knew and old friends of my student days, the "old man" Madeira Keita, the left pillar of the Union Soudanaise, and one of my oldest friends in the region, a scientist from Niger, Abdou Moumouni. I made new friends among Malians and foreigners who had come to assist the new socialist experiment, Jean and Blanche Molle, Marcel Faure, the Portuguese comrade Rui da Nobrega and his family, the anti-Zionist Israeli Elie Lobel. I was accepted in the country as a comrade of the Union Soudanaise and shared the hopes and fears of its extreme left.

I worked at the planning ministry and tried to put the national accounts into a comprehensive and useful shape. I made an inventory of projects and tried to assess their worth and connection. I had a horror of being treated as an "expert" and tried rather to encourage dialogue between "us" as the technical team with some knowledge to contribute and the comrades who held political responsibility in the state and the party. I have a strong memory of these dialogues. Many of my Malian comrades became intimate friends. Our discussions were frank, honest, and intense. Many of the comrades had little formal training, but they felt that I shared their concerns. At a higher level in the state, ministers and president were not always receptive to our arguments—I was careful not to presume to offer "advice." I sometimes felt I was back in Nasser's Egypt, but without Egypt's powerful ingredient of anticommunism. In Mali, things went more smoothly but in the same direction. Many of the young new trainees from Europe made up for their lack of experience with leftist, ultranationalist language that was never critical. Most of them were quite at ease serving the reactionary regime that followed the fall of President Modibo Keita.

I will not name names or places. I knew the Malian officials of the period too well, and they trusted me. In Bamako, as in Cairo, Isabelle was a schoolteacher.

I began to feel that the Malian experiment was going nowhere, as it combined militant rhetoric about security brigades with increasing bureaucratic mediocrity. I began also to feel that as a foreigner I would no longer be understood. After discussion with my closest comrades on the left of the Union Soudanaise, I decided to move on. Where? Similar situations in the Arab and African world would have the same result. I was thinking that after all I should go into university research and teaching.

I was then offered an appointment at the African Institute for Economic Development and Planning (IDEP),
which had just been established by the UN in Dakar. I
accepted.

My first spell with IDEP did not last long. As often
happens in this kind of institution, much depended on the
director. It was still the age of technical assistance, which
usually spells mediocrity and the unwitting implementation of pure neocolonialism. The last director at IDEP had
gone on to work with the International Monetary Fund.
IDEP was designed as a second-class training "school" for
planning techniques. It had not the slightest pretension to
a critical view. I tried to give my lectures on national
accounting and planning another approach. I drew on
actual cases in Mali, Guinea, Ghana, Egypt, the Maghreb
countries. I have kept the lecture notes, and they seem to
me reasonable. I was also studying the famous economic
"miracle" of the the Ivory Coast. The conclusions I reached
did not please the World Bank or the mediocre director of
IDEP. The Bank rushed to answer me in a glossy publication that cost a hundred times more than my study. The
Bank's conclusions, if read again today, would make
anyone with a sense of humor laugh, whereas my forecasts
have been confirmed in an even more disastrous reality.
The exercise brought me the director's total enmity. When
I decided to leave the institution, I took the precaution of
writing what I thought of it to the then UN Secretary
General, U Thant.

Meanwhile Jean Bénard had persuaded me to become
qualified as an economics teacher. I thought, why not? I
really had no time or desire to submit to the discipline—for
which I had little regard—of preparation for this kind of
high-level competition. I did so, however, and passed at the
first attempt in 1966. The gates of French university teaching were opening wide before me. As was customary, I
took a first appointment in the provinces—in Poitiers, as it

happened—and this demanded several visits. I had the privilege of dividing my time between Poitiers and Dakar.

Then came 1968. I returned to Paris from Dakar on May 1 to begin my course in Poitiers on May 15. The summer holidays were spent elsewhere, and there I was. In the autumn, Paris VIII, the famous Vincennes campus, was created. I found an agreeable and useful place there and went on spending some time in France and some in Dakar.

My letter to the UN Secretary General was of similar tenor to the findings of a mission to evaluate IDEP. In 1970 I was offered an appointment as director of IDEP. I was in a position for a while to impose my views. I believed that it would be a brief while, as the system would not long allow a center to train Africans to have a critical and independent spirit. An old friend whose name I shall withhold told me it would be longer than I expected. He was right. During the first five years of my duties I was supported by Robert Gardiner, the executive secretary of the Economic Commission for Africa. He was a man for whom I had great respect because despite his conservatism he was always upright and dignified. His successor, Adebayo Adedeji, despite his nationalist rhetoric, could not resist the temptation to align with the adversaries of IDEP's role—the U.S. establishment, naturally, and some of its lackeys.

I remained director of IDEP from August 1970 to June 1980. I did not want to become a bureaucratic director and carried on teaching. I also continued to keep in touch with reality through study missions. I went on with my writings, as Chapter 6 will show.

My ambition was to change the "school" into a combined scholarship and research center. I wanted to make it a focus of Africa-wide debates, with an emphasis on the political economy of dependence, liberation, and social change and of world capitalism. I wanted IDEP to contribute to bringing Africa out of neocolonial isolation. For this purpose I organized the first large meetings between intellectuals from Africa and counterparts in Latin America in 1972 and in Asia in 1974.

At IDEP I met Roland Ga Kwame Amoa, who shared my ideas and became a friend. I always admired among his qualities his great diplomacy (I told him he could have been the foreign minister of a great power). I brought to IDEP distinguished professors, such as Fawzy Mansour, Hector Silva Michelena, Oscar Braun, Norman Girvan, and some brilliant younger people, such as Bernard Founou-Tchuigoua, a loyal friend and associate in the running of the Third World Forum.

I believe IDEP played a useful role in the 1970s. We trained at least a thousand young Africans capable of critical judgment of "development" policies and programs. We also contributed to an active Africa-wide intellectual community. We decentralized the institute's work as much as possible. We held national or regional seminars. We reached out directly or indirectly to thousands of young people and hundreds of university teachers.

The ground was prepared to create from the IDEP nucleus other African institutions with more specific or general tasks. Three should be mentioned here. The Council for the Development of Economic and Social Research in Africa (CODESRIA), still based in Dakar, was housed at IDEP during the first seven difficult years after its launching, when it had no secure funding. I was for three years its first executive secretary, and when this was no longer needed I handed over the reins to Abdalla Bujra. I started ENDA (Program for Environment and Development in Africa) as a UN and IDEP project concerned with environmental issues in 1972, when their significance was not widely understood. I handed it over to Jacques Bugnicourt, and ENDA later stood on its own. Finally a few friends and I launched the Third World Forum (TWF) at Santiago de Chile in 1973 (obviously in President Salvador Allende's term) and it went on to become a great focus of debate. Again I located the TWF's African Office at IDEP, until I left the institute.[7]

The enemy never stopped trying to sabotage our efforts. Officials—Africans alas—of the UN system, too mediocre to refuse the behest of the reactionary establishment of the "first world," never ceased spending their time sabotaging IDEP. I knew they would succeed in the end. I realized I would spend most of my time in the bureaucratic battle to ensure the institute's survival and could not ensure its development. I thought it best to leave and carry the battle on from another platform that could be expanded. I gave up directorship of IDEP in 1980. The TWF's African office was housed temporarily in the independent CODESRIA building from 1980 to 1983, and then in its own modest offices.

Since 1980 I have directed the TWF's African office, with Bernard Founou, who joined me. The TWF is established in Dakar, where our proposal was welcomed by President Senghor and then by President Abdou Diouf in a genuinely democratic spirit. We owe them much. A simple tolerance of social reflection is unfortunately not the commonest thing, especially in third world countries, whether they have right-wing or left-wing governments.

The search for funding has not always been easy, but it has been achieved. I must say that I found the best response in Sweden. I explained my plan of action to Prime Minister Olof Palme, and he at once gave me the go-ahead. The Swedish Agency for Research Co-operation with Developing Countries (SAREC) has always been exceptionally generous, betting on the TWF before it had proved itself, as it has now done, I trust.

The forum has gradually become a center for significant research projects and a debating society of the kind that existed in nineteenth-century Europe. It might be described as a third world Society for International Development

(SID). (The real SID is dominated by the conservative establishment in the World Bank.) It answered a need that no other institution met. Academic research is pursued in many universities. Governments and so-called development agencies prefer action research. Debate is necessary to situate the research conclusions in a broader context and to inspire the men and women politicians, in government or opposition, and the intelligentsia of the people's institutions. The TWF tries to respond to this need by arranging meetings and debates on all aspects of the development crisis, economic and social, political, ideological, and cultural. The outcome of this debate, always critical but open-minded and nonsectarian, has been shown in numerous publications in several of the languages used in Africa, including some fifty books and several hundred articles.

I have tried to follow the evolution of the crisis in the African and Arab worlds, the response from the authorities, the alternatives proposed by parties, organizations, and individuals concerned with improving conditions for the ordinary people and with their empowerment. Our office in Dakar coordinates the research and discussion networks developed in a similar framework in Latin America and Asia.

I have been involved for several decades in political life in the third world, especially in the Arab and African worlds. My activities have brought me into close touch with many liberation organizations, political parties, and governments. I meet the leaders, sometimes at the highest level. I have been approached by some and have discussed with them and sometimes offered my opinion. I have agreed to do so on principle without necessarily accepting the effectiveness of the action, whenever I felt that the request came from a desire to promote national positions, to resist imperialist pressure, and to encourage progress favorable to the ordinary people. I do not believe the time has come to leave to the succeeding generations information for their analyses, still less additional material for the historians, that would be highly subjective personal assessments of institutions and the men who have led them (there were few women among these African personalities). I am content to offer my personal assessment of the political lines pursued and the underlying analysis. I believe that to go further would endanger the trust these personalities have placed in me.

6

Critical Analysis of Development Theory, 1955-1990

In Chapters 3 and 4 I have shown the steps involved in forming a theory of polarizing accumulation on a world scale. This theory shares some of the observations, analyses, and conclusions of other theories and views of the globalization of capitalism. I have even been classified among the authors of the dependency school and of the world-system school, with some justification. I believe, however, that the theory of polarizing accumulation I have outlined is unique.

I put systematic emphasis on polarization as the inherent result of actually existing world capitalism rather than an epiphenomenon of specific conditions in various historical societies. This has never, in my view, been a bar to case studies. On the contrary, I have based my theoretical propositions on case studies. I have, however, always sought to go beyond the particular to reach the level of abstraction demanded by the formulation of the general tendencies of capitalism. As Aidan Foster-Carter has shown in examining my early published work, the empirical Samir Amin leads over the theoretical.[1] The case studies I cite in this chapter stretch from 1955 to 1990 and coincide with the development of my theory of capitalist accumulation on a world scale. I tried to avoid two pitfalls: a theoretical formulation divorced from reality and a range of empirical analyses devoid of any theoretical hypothesis.

The case studies have always sought to criticize the concepts and practices of the so-called development policies implemented in the third world in the third of a century under consideration. I have never hesitated to sketch in or explain what I believed to be the alternative to these concepts and practices. I have never sought to build a wall between scientific analysis and the political line needed to change the world. I have never tried to hide that I identified with the ordinary people who form the majority of humankind. I have explained a distinction between the concept of capitalist expansion and the concept of development. I have examined the latter critically and shown an alternative approach.

My position on the theory of capitalist accumulation led me at each step to reinterpret my reading of Marxism. I have not hesitated to raise new questions and to seek answers in the field of historical materialism. My concept of polarization (polarized accumulation inherent in actually existing capitalism) entailed a rereading of Marx and of historical Marxism: in fundamental conceptualization of the capitalist mode of production (commodity alienation, social integration through the market) in relation to polarization and its effects; in conceptions of "transition" beyond capitalism (the task of "building socialism") and a critique of its implementation in practice.

This analysis of the modern world challenged earlier formulations of historical materialism regarding: the character of the earlier systems and dynamic of change; the origins of capitalism and explanation of its early appearance in Europe; noneconomic aspects of social life in the earlier systems and in capitalism; the relationships between political power, ideology and culture, and reproduction of the economic system.

I shall not address all these issues in this chapter but stick to a critical analysis of development concepts and practices. I shall consider my contribution to the development of historical materialism in later chapters and I shall return to the challenge of polarization and the identification of a response, or issues of "transition," the prospects for socialism and delinking.

I shall not attempt to summarize in sequence the books and articles I have written on this subject over the past thirty-five years. It would be tedious and repetitive. I shall present the essence of the lessons I have drawn and cite my studies in terms of the countries and regions or themes addressed.

COUNTRIES AND REGIONS STUDIED

I developed my critique of development concepts and practices in close liaison with my own personal and professional experience as a so-called expert in one or other development agency. I was in Egypt from 1957 to 1960 and in Mali from 1960 to 1963, and in the 1960s and 1970s I went on missions to various African and Arab countries, including Algeria, Tunisia, Morocco, Guinea, Ghana, the Ivory Coast, Congo, Madagascar, Tanzania, and Burkina Faso.

As a planning economist I developed from 1957 to 1963 a yardstick for the articulation and projection of economic indicators appropriate for the kind of socioeconomic analysis that seemed necessary. It was not a case of everything being grist for the mill. Statistical sources were much less advanced than they are now. It was necessary to abstract the indicators that were meaningful for my analysis. I suggested a methodology based on income distribution and development finance that was usually neglected in the conventional approaches of development economists, in analyses of past data or projections in planning policies. I used the method to analyze the experience of Egypt, Mali, Guinea, the Ivory Coast, and other West African and Central African countries, and Madagascar. I also used this method in my teaching material on national accounting and planning.

EGYPT

As an Egyptian citizen and a leftist militant from an early age I wrote between 1955 and 1962 a series of articles strongly critical of the concepts of Nasserism. At the end of my experience in Cairo from 1957 to 1960 I synthesized them in my pseudonymous book.[2]

My analysis went beyond the critique of Nasser's economic policy to analyze the historical roots of the Egyptian problem in the economic aspect of the development of capitalism in Egypt from 1880 to 1950, and in the social, political, ideological, and cultural aspects as well. My main conclusions differed from the ideas that then prevailed in Arab and Egyptian Marxism.

Capitalism had, in my view, totally upset the country's social structure, which no longer had anything "feudal" about it. Landholding had become essentially capitalist in nature and provided the axis for the local bourgeoisie, which was reactionary and allied to world imperialism. The industrial bourgeoisie, tentatively emerging after 1920, was nothing more than a branch of the same comprador bourgeoisie. Egypt had no national bourgeoisie in the Marxist sense of the term—that is, no anti-imperialist bourgeoisie.

The anti-imperialist political parties and movements had never been genuine representatives of the national bourgeoisie, or a popular alliance of workers and peasants, or a supposed petty bourgeoisie; rather they were movements of the intelligentsia. This shifted the debate on their project for society to ideology and culture, and to their concept of modernization, the external challenge, and the role of power. I included in this category the old pre-Wafd nationalist party, the Free Officers, and even the Communist movement.

I tried to link recent history to the more distant nineteenth-century reign of Mohamed Ali and the Nahda renaissance. I produced a hypothesis, which I applied to Egypt and to the whole Arab and Islamic world.[3]

I judged Nasserism harshly as I believed it had exhausted the potential for its statist bourgeois national project in Egypt and the Arab world in a very brief space of time. According to the conventional wisdom from 1957 to 1967, the project was the beginning of the building of socialism, whose first step took the form of the "noncapitalist road." I saw this as a form of capitalist development integrated into the new globalization that was crystallizing at the time and based on the industrialization of the third world. I believed that it would end as it did in Sadat's *infitah* open door. I stressed the reactionary side of Nasser's ideology paving the way for the later rise of Islamic fundamentalism.[4]

THE ARAB WORLD AS A WHOLE

I made an economic analysis of other Arab experiences using the method I had devised from my experiences in Egypt and West Africa: in the Maghreb; Syria and Iraq; and in the Arab world generally.[5]

I always came to approximately the same conclusion despite the particularities of the historical and political patterns. In the Maghreb, plebeian Algeria was emerging from the war of liberation, bourgeois Tunisia was emerging from the Bourguiba philosophy, and aristocratic and archaic Morocco was engaging in the politics of development. Land reform in Syria and Iraq redistributed income in favor of the less indigent half of the rural community, as in Egypt, and encouraged the expansion of kulak-style agrarian capitalism. Syria followed a more classical model of industrialization, with stress on import-substitution industries. Iraq was closer to the Gulf model and stressed heavy chemical industry based on oil. In all cases, the social and political achievements were limited.

Some general conclusions appeared important to me. A failure of agricultural development was manifest everywhere in increasing food dependency for a mix of reasons. One major factor was common: without a genuine delinking of internal relative prices (founded on a national and popular law of value) from those of the world market, the rewards for peasant labor remained lower than those for urban labor and development of this handicapped agriculture was obstructed and could not keep pace with rising needs. This is a manifestation of the urban preponderance in the hegemonic blocs.

Industrialization was dependent on external technology and finance even in the public sector and was also not delinked. Industrialization remained trapped in the conventional option between import substitution and exports instead of being related to a popular rural and urban demand which remained secondary, and therefore inequality in income distribution was reproduced. Industrialization was soon stifled as demand came from an increase in tertiary incomes more than from agriculture and industry.

This development model brought increasing vulnerability through food shortages and foreign debt. I concluded that it was part of transnational globalization and made no contribution to autocentric construction in the transition to socialism. I criticized the terminology of the "noncapitalist road."

The development policies that were implemented in this framework widened internal social polarization. To a more striking degree than in the capitalist West, scarce resources in skilled labor and capital were used to meet the consumption needs of the privileged classes. The more one moves up the scale of per capita income among Arab countries, the more distorted is the pattern of use of scarce resources.

The policies revealed the deep link between the degree of the transnationalization and the internal social polarization peculiar to the peripheries of the system and their regressive social character. They produced some modest achievements, but did not allow the region to join the ranks of newly industrialized countries or industrial exporters such as Korea.

I always felt the need to offer an alternative to the policies I criticized. The proposals I made may seem highly "technocratic" to a reader. I am thinking of my conclusion in 1970 when I looked twenty years ahead to the economic potential of the Maghreb in 1990. I had a vision of a region delinked, modernized, autocentric, embarked on agricultural development, and in the early stages of successful industrialization, based on an income distribution that wiped out the intolerable inequalities inherited from peripheral capitalism.[6] I believed it had to be shown that there was a realistic alternative policy. A projection naturally assumes that the real problems of the social content of power have been resolved. The pace of the results on paper is never realistic. This illusion reinforces the debatable notion that it is almost entirely a matter of catching up, when catching up is only part of the question—the real issue is starting something different. I later considered how the ambiguity could be cleared up.

SUB-SAHARAN AFRICA

I had to look back at the colonial legacy when judging the "new" development policies implemented in independent Africa after 1960.[7] This shaded the judgments on the supposed new age of development as it broadly followed the models of the previous colonial capitalist expansion.

Colonial exploitation had taken different forms which I finally divided into three macroregions: Africa of the colonial trade economy, Africa of the concession-owning companies, and Africa of the labor reserves.[8] I noted further that independence marked the transition to a new stage of peripheral capitalist development.[9] In the colonial period, growth was almost exclusively driven by external demand. With import-substitution industrialization, demand comes partly from within as the middle classes benefit from this kind of development. I wondered whether an association between low wages and comparatively high productivity in the new industry (I rejected the still-fashionable thesis of a labor aristocracy in Africa) would allow accelerated industrialization through import substitution and runaway export industry. I put the hypothesis forward, but it was contradicted by events. The colonial policy based on extensive agriculture has remained the rule, and the marked anti-industry prejudice has been sustained by the behavior of the European community. I noted too that those countries that did persist in industrialization inevitably had to resort to statist forms at this stage. This was in no way a step on the transition to socialism but a step to capitalist expansion. This observation was strongly rejected at the time by most of the African and foreign left, but I was subsequently proven correct. I noted finally that colonization, far from favoring the development of an Africa bourgeoisie, had choked off its potential whenever the development represented a political threat.[10]

My analysis stressed consideration over a long period, sometimes dating as far back as the nineteenth century when this was necessary for an understanding of the structures bequeathed to the new states (Senegal, Dahomey-Benin, Congo, Ghana) and to the Africa of the colonial trade economy (the Ivory Coast and the Sahel countries). The model that was generally followed after 1960 seemed to me to be at its last gasp and to lead to disaster in a double crisis of public finance and external debt even before the initial step of industrialization was taken. For me, the fourth world phenomenon hove into sight in 1960.

It was necessary to pay close attention to the apparent differences between the economic policies of the various countries on the continent. I shall make some brief points.

Substantial mineral resources (in Guinea, Mauritania, and Gabon and Congo later on) that brought the state some financial leeway would delay, but not prevent, the reckoning. My critique of Guinea, which was broadly regarded as too harsh at the time, was subsequently borne out.

Areas that were lagging behind in the colonial times before 1960 had a margin for catching up. This was my explanation for the Ivorian "miracle," which I compared with the previous development of Ghana. I expected from the beginning that it would soon end, and this has been the case. The World Bank was still pouring out unreserved praise in the 1970s, and its perspective seemed superficial and mistaken. (The World Bank has yet to confess its error.)

The apparent unity of the colonial space was not really founded on a genuine integration of the regions. It was a matter of the juxtaposition of regions separately integrated into the metropolitan space. The break-up into independent states was feasible and easy, and even supported by the embryonic new ruling class associated with independence. The break-up made for intolerable conditions for some countries (Dahomey-Benin, Niger, the hinterland of the former French Equatorial Africa) and turned others into second-rank peripheries supplying the first-rank peripheries with labor (Upper Volta/Burkina Faso) or cheap foodstuffs (Mali's livestock).

The problem of internal migration throughout West Africa came into this framework. I noted the magnitude of the overall migration flows which changed the proportions of the population of the hinterland to that of the coastal areas from 2:1 in 1920 to 1:1 in 1970—and the negative impact on the regions of emigration impoverished by the transfer of value concealed in this movement of labor.[11] I discussed the migratory phenomenon (like the demographic phenomenon considered below) as an element in the process of proletarianization and linked it to capitalist agricultural expansion. I noted in passing that Nigeria, where each of the great regions in the north, west, and east had its own reserves for proletarianization and the associated internal migration, had a potential for less difficult autocentric development.

The overall model for regional development resulting from colonial history and policies after 1960 seemed absurd. It sacrificed the great regions of the interior and the immense potential of the great rivers that crossed them. The need for continental development that Africa's geography cried out for was consistently ignored. Colonization and the neocolonial system substituted artificial, mediocre, or ludicrous plans. In Senegal, for example, no attention was given to the potential for intensive irrigated agriculture along the Senegal River and in Casamance, combined with mixed farming and livestock in the region that had been assigned to groundnuts under colonization. Overexploitation of labor and soil exhaustion from the groundnut economy prepared the way for desertification and fourth world status.

I was understandably sympathetic to attempts to escape the colonial and neocolonial impasse. I did not hesitate to make a personal commitment to these attempts in Mali from 1960 to 1963, in Ghana under Nkrumah and Rawlings, and in Congo, Burkina Faso, and Tanzania. I return to my harsh criticisms of the policies being implemented. Often I expressed those criticisms in a purposefully technocratic language. I had to use a language that could persuade decisionmakers that there was a better way.

SOUTHERN AFRICA

Southern Africa has its own particular characteristics, which I studied.[12] I noted that the pursuit of capitalist accumulation in South Africa necessarily implied South African expansionism into southern Africa. The intervention and destabilization policies were part of this logic. The course of events showed that South Africa's ambition to become a regional NIC failed.[13] Does this rule out the neocolonial solution whose danger and likelihood for South Africa after Zimbabwe I sketched?

BROAD PROBLEMS IDENTIFIED

The development challenge facing the third world seemed to revolve around the necessary precondition of an agrarian and peasant revolution—and I insist on the peasant component. I see this as a correct expression of an analysis in terms of historical materialism and not development techniques. It requires consideration of the precolonial social formations of the past and the attitude for or against imperialism of the hegemonic social blocs in the present. I examined these issues in the context of Egypt, the Arab world, and sub-Saharan Africa, to which I shall return below.

Drawing on the findings of my case studies, I wrote a series of articles that addressed the problematic of agricultural revolution and autocentric industrialization.[14]

In the history of the development of capitalism in the centers, the agricultural revolution preceded or accompanied the Industrial Revolution. Different forms of bourgeois revolution were required according to the presence or absence of a peasant aspect.

The ideology of historical socialism that Sovietism inherited regarded the peasants as a reserve to finance industrialization. This view canceled out the possibility of real development because of the economic distortion created by the failure of agricultural development and the political distortion created by breaching the worker-peasant alliance. This put into question the very idea of catching up that underlay the grim choice.

I started from Mao's proposition in "On the Ten Major Relationships," drawing on a critique of the Soviet experience. This implied rejecting the two other paths: the capitalist road of converting peasant-based subsistence agriculture to agribusiness and the Soviet road of creating cooperatives controlled and exploited by the state. It implied drawing on the inspiration of the Chinese communes, notwithstanding their shortcomings. It implied, therefore, industrialization at the service of agricultural development, which left behind the spurious bourgeois debate: import substitution or export industries.

My conclusions were based on a critique of the fashionable views of what I called bourgeois development ideology. This was seen in the Pearson reports and in the reports from CILSS (Permanent Interstate Committee for Drought Control in the Sahel) and the World Bank. Sometimes I worked from a critique of the national policies implemented here and there in the Arab world and sub-

Saharan Africa. I noted, for example, that the EEC had achieved its food self-sufficiency by a policy of delinking European agricultural prices from those of the world market. But it opposed any similar policy in the third world, which remained a prisoner of European and U.S. competition in the negotiations of the Uruguay round of the General Agreement on Tariffs and Trade!

Some particular issues of industrialization found their place in this analysis of nondelinked strategies—for instance, the outward-looking view of third world integration in the world minerals and energy markets, the issue of technology reduced to a spurious problem of transfer, and various writings on the major international negotiations.[15]

The population issue is inseparable from the challenge of capitalist expansion. Malthus is always brought back at the moment of transition from precapitalist systems (characterized by matching low rates of growth in population and agricultural productivity) to the capitalist system (characterized by improved population growth and greater agricultural productivity combined with still greater industrial productivity). Hence in the transition, industrialization must support agricultural breakthrough and the appropriate policy of delinking and a popular hegemonic social alliance. I contrasted this analysis with the conventional approach to demography.[16]

I include in the framework of a delinked, autocentric strategy, with a popular content and socialist vocation, the issues of regional integration and cooperation. I began from an analysis of South-South trade;[17] the language, practices, and proposals of cooperation;[18] and a consideration of how the franc zone operated.[19]

I observed that inter-African trade, like South-South trade, was complementary to unequal North-South relations, and it was necessary to change it so that it gradually became at least a partial alternative to unequal relations. It was essential to build autonomous, delinked space based on the planned implementation of complementarities, and not on the illusory common market.

The colonial legacy of the franc zone could not be regarded as positive in the necessary reconstruction. I favored gradual reform, which seemed to me politically feasible and a step forward, but it has not been undertaken.

SOCIETY, STATE, POLITICS, AND ECONOMICS

I never believed that the critique of so-called development experiences could remain confined to economics. The political and social dynamic was always at issue.

THE ARAB WORLD

My six main theses clashed with opinions current in the 1970s among Arab Marxists.[20] I envisaged the new industrial bourgeoisie and its kulak ally forced by imperialism to pursue a line that would end in a neocomprador role. Soviet support might be defensible as international policy but did not justify the so-called noncapitalist road, and building Arab unity required a recognition of the diversity of the countries and a popular front free of the illusion that the Arab bourgeoisies, as statist radicals, could achieve the goal.

I wrote in the wake of the 1967 defeat and in the conclusion examined several scenarios, highlighting the possibility of rapid, positive response from a people's power alliance to challenge the neocomprador role. When facts proved different, I thought it necessary to explain the failure by bringing into my analysis more of the cultural and ideological aspect of the problem.[21]

I recently tried to synthesize my findings, analyzing the long historical cycle beginning from 1800 for Egypt, 1919 for the Mashreq, and 1960 for the Maghreb, and petering out in the 1970s and 1980s as a succession of attempts to build a bourgeois national state.[22] I highlighted the right-left clash that had broken the unanimity of the national liberation movement and the permanent crisis it entailed. I saw the populist outcome of the 1950s and 1960s not as an appropriate solution to the crisis but as an attempt to suppress its manifestation. The political and ideological vacuum caused by suppression entailed in turn the impasse of Islamic traditionalism. In objective terms, the populist episode ended in further incorporation of the Arab world in globalization. In this globalization, the Arab world is not grouped with the NICs, because its essential role for imperialism is as a strategically placed oil producer. I also considered the national question and minorities. The analysis of the Arab world was extended to a comparison with the experience of Kemalist Turkey.[23]

I should mention that these analyses of the modern period are connected in my mind to the analyses of the earlier periods. I thought it particularly useful to stress the relations between the Arab and Islamic East and medieval Europe, and the reversal of these relations following the crystallization of European capitalism.[24]

The region's strategic position highlighted the role of Israel and to the global perceptions and strategies of the United States, the USSR, and the European countries.[25]

SUB-SAHARAN AFRICA

My analysis of sub-Saharan Africa is contained in four

articles cited earlier.[26] I did not take the fashionable eth-
nological approach. I began my reading of African community formations on principles of historical materialism,
and analyzed the decline associated with colonial destruction of the ancient states and the emergence of wage and
pseudo-feudal forms of exploitation of the peasants. I went
on to open the debate about future options: should one
encourage the decline of the village community and
strengthen the commodity peasant economy? Would it be
possible to constrain the differentiations that agrarian
capitalism was bound to bring? How? Could one bypass
this step and go from the traditional village community to
a socialist cooperative?

On the national question in the modern period, I noted
that central capitalism was an integrating force but
peripheral capitalism disintegrated society and made national consciousness virtually impossible. I considered the
issue of "ethnicity" in Africa on this basis.[27]

I extended my critique of development policies to other
acute problems in Africa. I looked at democracy and
criticized the fashionable Weberian theses.[28] I examined the
difficulties of democracy as stemming not from traces of
the past but from the contradictions of peripheral
capitalism.

I saw the relations between the EEC and the ACP group
as central to the turning of Africa into a fourth world
phenomenon.[29]

I suggested that local and regional disputes in Africa were
a reflection of the USSR's and local ruling classes' conflict
with imperialism and the strategies of imperialism.[30]

ALTERNATIVES IN DELINKING

In the twenty years since 1970 I have given much attention to analyzing the unfolding structural crisis of the world system. I shall not repeat what I said in Chapter 4 but restrict myself to complementary aspects concerned with the collective strategy of the Group of 77 in major international negotiations and the political intervention strategies in North-South and East-West relations.[31]

I have already said that the NIEO proposal was aimed at modifying the rules of the game to give capitalist development in the peripheries a second chance. As the strategy was in contradiction with an autocentric strategy of delinking, it was bound to fail.

I also criticized the approach and proposals of the Group of 77 in major negotiations, especially in the UN Commission on Trade and Development (UNCTAD). On the basis of the 1967 Algiers Charter and 1971 Lima Declaration, I noted that the Group of 77 was demanding the opening of markets in the north for its members' industrial exports, more equitable prices for raw materials, a more appropriate international monetary system with a link between the creation of international liquidity and development finance, and a code of conduct for technology transfer. These demands are perfectly reasonable as long as they are accompanied by a preference for participation in the world system over delinking. Rejection of these demands acknowledges that delinking is the only realistic alternative and that reform of the world system is utopian.

I commented too that the analyses of the Group of 77 on the so-called less developed countries (LDCs) lacked scientific rigor. I observed that the LDCs formed a heterogeneous category embracing countries scarcely integrated into the world system, peripheries of peripheries and countries destroyed by integration at an earlier stage bypassed by capitalist evolution.

Before considering the alternative, I shall summarize my assessment of the development record.[32] I concluded that the development efforts made in the two decades preceding the general crisis were well and truly within the ambit of globalization, and not a challenge to it. They were bound to be stifled soon, and this has been the case. I return briefly to the debates of the 1950s and 1960s with their two opposing theses. On one side was neocolonial liberalism and globalization through maximum openness to the logic of the world market's "development." On the other was radical nationalism through industrialization and modernization, hastened by active state intervention and modifying the structures of globalization in favor of third world countries and offering the prospect of catching up. I noted a common denominator of the two theses of right and left. Under the clear influence of Sovietism, the prevailing leftist thesis of the time stressed the priority for basic industry, as "industrializing industries" and regarded agriculture and the rural community as essentially a reserve whose purpose was to finance industrialization. The matter became clear with the Maoist explanation "On the Ten Major Relationships" and the Cultural Revolution. From 1966 on, the fraction of the left to which I belonged abandoned all the ambiguities of the discourse of Sovietism. Later events—"maldevelopment"—proved us right. Recognition of this tolled the death knell of a development ideology that had dominated preceding decades in its dual form of neocolonial liberalism and Sovietism.

As always, my critique of the concepts and practices of development was complemented by the proposal of an alternative.[33] I shall summarize the direction my thinking took on various aspects of the alternative.

I defined delinking as the submission of external relations to the logic of internal development, the opposite of structural adjustment of the peripheries to the demands of the polarizing worldwide expansion of capital. I explained the distinction in terms of the law of value.[34] My position is illustrated by a comparison of capitalist development strategies at the center and the periphery. An autocentric strategy always entails active state intervention aiming at a favorable position in the international division of labor through a mixture of association and dissociation.

Two contrasting positions on the social content of development have gradually crystallized since the 1960s. In the Soviet experience, the aim of catching up gradually eclipsed that of building an alternative society. Delinking had been deployed for this purpose and had produced a Soviet bourgeoisie. The speeding up of the change to reintegrating the country into the world system and the abandonment of delinking did not ensure that the country would avoid peripheralization. Even more in the third world, the usual result for countries that declared their aim of building modern, self-reliant national economies but did not genuinely delink was a return to a comprador role. I concluded from this twofold experience that the effectiveness of the delinking strategy depended on the social aspect of the authority implementing it. The strategy is effective only when it is based on the least unequal income distribution possible.[35] History shows us that it is impossible to "catch up" within the framework of world capitalism, and that late-arrival bourgeoisies cannot imagine not being integrated into a world system of which they are beneficiaries. Delinking can serve only alternative development peculiar to a very long transition beyond capitalism.

I turned my attention to deepening the debate on the transition through a critique of radical third world experiences, the USSR experience and the propositions of Maoism.[36] By the mid-1980s I had reached a new conclusion: historical Marxism had underestimated the gravity of the problems caused by global polarization and posed the issue of the transition in the incorrect terms of bourgeois revolution or socialist revolution. The real question on history's agenda was a very long evolution beyond capitalism, of a national and popular character, based on delinking and a recognition of the genuine conflict between the trend toward capitalism and the aspiration for socialism.

The issue of building a social base for a national and popular alliance was one of my foremost concerns. I examined the issue of democratization and the special role of the intelligentsia from that perspective, and considered the problematic as defined in new terms.[37] The issues concerning the world order were addressed in relation to the delinked and democratic national strategy that was necessary. In articles on the struggle to build a polycentric world, I stressed my critique of European policies, which were always wishy-washy and negative regarding African and Arab unity.[38] In my most recent writings I have tried to incorporate the new strategic aspects of the redeployment of U.S. hegemonic ambitions.[39]

Finally, I defined the aims of rebuilding what I have called Socialism III on the foundations of an internationalism of peoples. This demands a shift to wage hegemony in the most advanced societies and to popular and national hegemony in the others. This stand does not put me among the third worldists, as many of my superficial critics concluded, but shows my fundamental stance as a universalist internationalist.

7

The System in Crisis: A Critique of Sovietism, 1960–1990

Except for individuals with a natural disposition to prophesy, nobody can pretend not to have been somewhat taken aback by the sudden and total collapse of the political systems of Eastern Europe and the USSR. Now that the surprise factor is gone, it is useful to look back at the analyses of these systems produced over some thirty years. At the risk of sounding pretentious, I may say that since 1960 I have been part of a small current on the left that had broadly foreseen what came to a climax between 1989 and 1991. Of course, the collapse we thought highly likely was not the only possible outcome of the crisis of the Soviet system. I do not believe in any unfailing linear determinism in history. The contradictions running through every society always find their resolution in diverse responses according to their class content. It was always possible that the Soviet regime might fall to the right (as happened) or evolve (or fall) to the left. The latter possibility has been ruled out for the immediate future but remains on the agenda of history, not only because there is never an end to history but also because I doubt that the right-wing solution in the making will stabilize the societies of the East, even in the medium term.

In rereading what I have written on these topics from 1960 to 1990, I shall not fail to point out the weaknesses and errors brought out by later evolution.

The analyses, judgments, and even forecasts must be put into a context, although they were always more or less affected by the circumstances of the changes under consideration. During these thirty years the Soviet system has evolved and sought to respond to the crisis and gone through various phases.

From Stalin's death in 1953, and especially from the Twentieth Congress in 1956 to the fall of Khrushchev in 1964, the period was marked by a first attempt to recover from Stalinism and by the open ideological and political dispute between Moscow and Beijing. The next period of so-called Brezhnev glaciation (i.e., immobilist strategy) lasted until the arrival of Gorbachev in 1985. Gorbachev's attempt at perestroika after 1985 ended within a few years in the collapse from 1989 to 1991.

China was at the same time also seeking alternative responses to the problem of building socialism—in its own terminology. There was the Maoist attempt from 1961 to 1976, culminating in the Cultural Revolution from 1966 and the gradual slide which led to Deng Xiaoping's economic and political strategy characteristic of the 1980s.

The evolutions and successive phases had to be articulated on those operating at a world level. This meant capitalist expansion and the building of the EEC in Europe, and competition between the United States, Japan, and Europe. It meant military balances between the two superpowers and political responses in the arms race. In the Brezhnev period it meant Soviet initiatives toward the third world and conflict with China on the one hand, and on the other, U.S. Cold War strategies, including Star Wars preparations after 1980. Internal options and international policies were intertwined during these thirty years.

Of course, the Soviet system does not date from 1960 and our reflections are based on our analysis of both the 1917 Russian Revolution and the Chinese Revolution, Leninism, Maoism, and Stalinism. It is not our intention to propose a new reading of the seventy-five years of Soviet history. I shall not expound on the forty-year period from 1917 to

1957, when successive phases of the evolution of the Soviet system were linked to various moments of world history, or on postwar Stalinism and the early Cold War.

I must add a personal note. As an Egyptian I lived through the Nasserist experience, and from 1960 on I saw that Nasserism would lead to what developed openly from 1971 as Sadat's *infitah* open door: the return to the cradle of compradorization. I felt the same anxieties in the first wave of other "socialist" experiences in Africa—in Algeria, Mali, Guinea, and Ghana—in the first half of the 1960s. The judgment that was at the time rejected by the great majority of the Egyptian and international left led me to follow the Communist Party of China's criticism of the Soviet leadership. The criticism was made in veiled terms from 1957 to 1958, then openly in the "Letter in Twenty-Five Points" in 1964, and most visibly in the Cultural Revolution after 1966. It was the beginning of a correct response to the "crisis of socialism" before this became a popular theme in the West in 1968.

After 1960 certainly, and even after 1957, I ceased to consider Soviet society as socialist or that the power of the workers was "deformed by bureaucracy," in the famous Trotskyist expression. I had from the beginning regarded the ruling exploiting class (and I do mean *class*) as a bourgeoisie. This class, the *nomenklatura*, saw itself in the mirror of a West it aspired to replicate. This is what Mao had perfectly expressed in a phrase spoken in 1963 when he was addressing cadres of the Chinese Communist Party: "You [meaning the Chinese party cadres like those of the USSR] have constructed a bourgeoisie. Do not forget: the bourgeoisie does not want socialism, it wants capitalism."

I drew the logical conclusions from this analysis of the party and the attitude of the masses toward the authorities. To me it was obvious that the masses did not recognize themselves in the authorities, although they continued to proclaim themselves socialist, but they saw them, rather, as their true social adversaries—and rightly so. In these circumstances, the party was a long-moldering corpse that had become an instrument of social control over the masses exercised by the exploiting ruling class. The Communist Party, crowning the work of the repressive institutions such as the KGB, organized a network of clients among the people, through control and distribution of all social benefits, even the slightest, thus paralyzing their potential revolt. This kind of party in no way differs from the many one-party systems in the third world playing the same role (under the label of radical nationalism such as Nasserism, the Algerian FLN, the Ba'ath, and the long train of parties in office in Mali, Guinea, Ghana, Tanzania, etc., or without this label in the countries opting openly for capitalism, in the Ivory Coast and elsewhere). It is a general pattern suitable for situations where the emergent bourgeoisie has not yet established its ideological hegemony ("the ideology of the ruling class is the dominant ideology in society," Marx said about mature capitalism) and does not appear to exercise legitimate power (this would require a consensus established by the society's adherence to the ideology of its ruling class).

This kind of exercise of power, which fragments the masses through clientship, has a depoliticizing effect whose harm should not be underestimated. Events have now shown that in the USSR the depoliticization was of such breadth that the masses believe that the regime they are rid of was socialist, and ingenuously accept that capitalism is better.

All the elements of the system collapsed like a house of cards as soon as the leaders lost state power. Nobody was prepared to risk their lives to defend an apparatus of this kind. That is why struggles at the top in this kind of party always take the form of palace revolutions, with the grass roots unfailingly accepting those who become winners. I was not surprised by the instant conversion of Nasser's socialist union to Sadatism, nor by the spontaneous disap-pearances of other parties of the same flavor in many third world countries. I was no more surprised by the passive-ness displayed by "millions" of Soviet Communists after 1989.

Even if it was clear to me that Soviet society was not socialist, it always seemed to me much more difficult to describe it in positive terms.

I shall not repeat the reasons that made me refuse to believe that fundamental principles of socialism were being implemented, as I have explained them many times. For me socialism means more than the abolition of private property (a negative characteristic); it has a positive mean-ing of alternative labor relations other than those defining wage status, alternative social relations allowing society as a whole (and not an apparatus functioning on its behalf) to control its social future. This in turn means a democracy far more advanced than the best bourgeois democracy. In none of these ways was Soviet society different from industrial bourgeois society, and when it moved away from its original goals, it was worse, as its autocratic practice brought it closer to the prevailing model in the areas of peripheral capitalism.

I refused to describe the USSR as capitalist, although its ruling class was in my view bourgeois. My argument was that capitalism means the dispersal of the property of capital as the basis of competition, and that state centraliza-tion of this property commands a different logic of ac-cumulation. At the political level, I argue that the 1917 revolution was not a bourgeois revolution because of the character of the social forces who were its authors and because of the ideology and social project of its leading forces. This is no mean consideration.

I do not attach much significance to a positive description of the system. I have used for the purpose various terms such as "state capitalism" and "state monopoly capitalism," whose ambiguities I criticized, and finished up with the neutral term "Soviet mode of production." What seemed to me more important was the question of the origins, formation, and evolution of the system and, within this framework, its future.

I was not one of those who always regretted the 1917 revolution. ("It did not have to happen, because the objective conditions for the building of socialism did not exist; it was necessary to stop at the bourgeois revolution.") In my view, the worldwide expansion of capitalism is polarizing, and it is inevitable that the people who are its victims—on the periphery of the system—should revolt against its consequences. One can only support the people in their revolt. To stop at the bourgeois revolution is to betray those peoples, since the necessarily peripheral capitalism that would follow does not provide acceptable responses to the problems that motivated the revolt.

The Russian and Chinese revolutions opened a long transition whose outcome is unknown. The dynamic of their evolution may lead to central or peripheral capitalism, and both within the society and on a world scale it may encourage progress toward socialism. What is important is to analyze the objective direction of the advance. Along with a minority of the Communist left, I continue to support the two theses that seemed to me important in analyzing Soviet evolution.

Collectivization as implemented by Stalin after 1930 broke the worker-peasant alliance of 1917 and, by reinforcing the state's autocratic apparatus, opened the way to the formation of a "new class": the Soviet state bourgeoisie.

Because of some of its own historical limitations, Leninism had unwittingly prepared the ground for this fatal choice. I mean that Leninism had not broken radically with the economism of the Second International (of the Western labor movement, it must be said): its concept of the social neutrality of technology is evidence of this.

A society embarking on long transition faces contradic-tory demands. On the one hand, it must catch up, in the plain and simple sense of developing the productive forces. On the other hand, in its tendency to socialism it offers the alternative of building a society free of economistic aliena-tion. The latter characteristically sacrifices the two sources of wealth: the human being reduced to labor power and nature regarded as the inexhaustible object of human exploitation. Can it be done? I always thought the answer was yes, but with great difficulty: a pragmatic compromise to move gradually in the promising direction of the alter-native. The economism of Leninism contained the seed of a choice that would gradually make the goal of catching up triumph over the goal of the alternative.

My early adherence to Maoism and to the Cultural Revolution, which I do not repudiate, stems from this analysis. (I was astonished that Lenin had been surprised by Kautsky's betrayal in 1914.) I supported the thesis that Mao established a genuine return to a Marxism that had been distorted by the Western labor movement (and imperialism has its share of responsibility in this drift) even before it was distorted, as it still is partly, by Leninism.

Maoism offered a critique of Stalinism from the left, while Khrushchev made one from the right. Khrushchev was saying that insufficient concessions have been made to the economic constraints in the technological and scien-tific revolution and globalization and to the political im-plications of giving more authority to the enterprise directors, namely the Soviet bourgeoisie. Khrushchev was saying that in these circumstances we would catch up more quickly. Mao was saying that at every step the final goal must be remembered. This was the real meaning of "put-ting politics in command" (a meaning that has nothing to do with the facile accusation of voluntarism). To avoid losing sight of the final goal, Maoism insisted on equality between workers and peasants (essential in China, but equally so in the Russia of 1930) to strengthen and not break their alliance. I explained the goal in terms of what law of value to implement: (1) to surrender to that governing worldwide capitalism and accept thereby peripheral capitalist development; or (2) to envisage building an autocentric national economy, delinked from the world system but analogous to that of advanced capital (the law of value governing the Soviet statist mode of production and creating a Soviet national bourgeoisie); or (3) to establish relations between the masses based on the law of value of the socialist transition.

Mao rightly believed, as later evolution in the USSR and China showed, that the question should be handled at the level of power: challenge the monopoly of the Communist Party, crucible of the new bourgeoisie. Hence the big-character poster launching the Cultural Revolution: "Bombard the Headquarters" (of the Communist Party). Was he wrong to believe that it was the only way to increase workers' control over society and to drive the bureaucracy into retreat? He did not believe that concessions to market laws—more power to directors of enterprises, more competition among enterprises—would advance the people's social power. Was he wrong? I am not saying that concessions should not be made to the market. The New Economic Policy had done this successfully in its time. It had to be done, and more bravely than it was, but there were other conditions.

It had to be accompanied by political democratization. The genuine powers of the workers had to be strengthened in this democracy against those of the bourgeois technocrats. The market had to be incorporated into a state policy strongly based on the law of value of the transition to socialism.

The Yugoslavs tried badly and too timidly: too great an opening to the exterior; too great concessions, worsening internal tendencies to inequality between the republics in the name of competitiveness; excessive decentralization, leaving the self-managed collectives in a situation of mutual competition. In the USSR, nothing had been done in this direction, or in China, except in the good intentions of the Maoist period later abandoned.

I still believe that Maoism was right, even if the later evolution in China seems to contradict this. The evolution does not contradict it but confirms it: concessions to capitalism strengthen the bourgeoisie and weaken the chances of the masses. It is doubtless acceptable and necessary, even today with hindsight, to open the debate on the historical limitations of Maoism as has been done for Lenin (insufficient break with economism) and even for Marx (underestimation of the polarization inherent in worldwide capitalist expansion).

The central issue concerning the Soviet mode of production was whether it was an unstable solution, characteristic of a transitional period that was evolving toward capitalism or socialism, or a new and stable mode that, despite its faults, indicated the future of other normal capitalist societies.

I offer a self-criticism on this point. I thought at one time, from 1975 to 1985, that the Soviet mode was a stable and advanced form of what the normal tendency of capital should engender elsewhere, by the very act of centralization of capital, leading from private monopoly to state monopoly. There were signs of this at the time. I am not referring to the apparent stability of Brezhnev's USSR. I am referring rather to the earlier theoreticians (Bukharin's theory on state monopoly capitalism) or to propositions of the time: the convergence of systems that Jan Tinbergen detected, bringing together not only the USSR and the advanced West, but also the advanced West and the USSR, and positions in this direction taken by the left-wing social democracies (in Sweden, for example, with the plan for trade unions to buy up industry), Eurocommunism, etc. It seemed that statist centralization of capital, by suppressing competition—and the opacity of the market—produced similarity in the systems of prices charged by the monopolies and those charged by Gosplan. This parallel evolution inaugurated a return to the dominance of ideology. This ideology was not a return to the metaphysical religions of the tributary age, but the ideology of triumphant commoditization. There was the strong image of George Orwell's *1984* (to whose revived reputation I contributed at the time), the analysis of the monolithic consensus in the supposedly liberal and democratic societies of the West in Herbert Marcuse's *One-Dimensional Man*, which reminded me of my reading of Karl Polanyi. Why not the statist mode as the highest form of capitalism? The Soviet mode foretold a grim future, despite its primitive shape. (How happy Stalin would have been to have the Cable News Network rather than the newspaper *Pravda* to mold monolithic opinion, as was shown in the Gulf War!)

I added the observation that in the bourgeois revolution the struggle of the peasants against the feudalists did not end in the victory of the oppressed, but in the rise of a third party: the bourgeoisie. Why should the battle of the workers (or wage earners) against the capitalists not become the business of the "new class"?

Events proved me wrong. The Soviet regime proved to be unstable, and the offensive of the worldwide right from 1980 was in the opposite direction: deregulation and privatization had their heyday.

I return to my self-criticism with a subtle distinction. Never mind that the Soviet model was incapable of becoming a definite alternative gradually copied by others. Events show that it was not. This may reflect only its own weaknesses. It does not mean that in other parts of the developed world, once the recent wave of liberal utopia is over, evolution may not follow a path mapped out by the old USSR.

I have returned to considerations remoter from the present and the instability of the transition in which the Soviet model indicates a historic cycle now complete. It seemed to me that the description "socialist phase" was more deceptive than useful. I accept that this might be described as primitive socialism. Even before the break-up of the Soviet system 1989 it seemed to me in recent years that it was more fruitful to describe the transition as "national and popular." This stressed the contradiction between the goals of this phase and the logic of worldwide capitalist expansion (a contradiction symbolized by the description as national, in reference to my concept of delinking). It stressed the contradictory content of the popular bloc, neither bourgeois nor proletarian with a socialist vocation. The long transition is by nature unstable. It may lead to capitalism, as happened in the USSR. It may lead somewhere else, and I shall return to this in the conclusion.

An assessment is needed of the Soviet cycle now completed. It is not positive overall, or negative. The USSR, and subsequently China and even the small countries of Eastern Europe, have built modern autocentric economies such as no country of peripheral capitalism has succeeded in doing. According to my analysis, this is because the Soviet bourgeoisie was produced by a popular and national, so-called socialist, revolution, whereas the bourgeoisies of the third world constituted in the wake of the worldwide expansion of capitalism are generally of a comprador nature. The ambiguous character of the socialist aspect of the revolution has shaped a society in which the workers have won social rights (the right to work and social welfare) that have no match even in developed central capitalism (where some of the rights were belatedly won by great struggle, usually after the world wars, in part because of the fear of Communism), and even more so in crude peripheral capitalism.

Today the overt capitalist option of the USSR and Eastern Europe returns to the agenda the peripheralization of their economy and society for which the popular classes (and even the local bourgeoisies) are unprepared by the depoliticization wrought by blind statist despotism. I had underestimated the depoliticization and the disastrous effects that have now become evident and thought that the peoples and ruling classes of the East would be able to control the evolution toward capitalism to which the latter aspired through reforms associated with the gradual passage to political democratization. I thought that in these circumstances the popular classes might bend the evolution toward the general advance of socialism. The socialist aspirations of workers for social rights and a more active role in the management of their workplace and country would be more evenly balanced with the demands of the market, including but not restricted to the aspirations of the bourgeoisie. A revived national popular alliance would reopen debate on socialism on a world scale in the West and on the periphery. I must offer a self-criticism on this point, as this prospect is now ruled out and the rightist evolution toward crude capitalism is irreversible. I may not be wrong in the long term, however, when the results of this peripheralization become evident, when the workers realize that the drastic fall in their standard of living is not a momentary sacrifice imposed by the transition.

The Soviet system long ago entered the phase of acute crisis, which has become terminal. The system failed repeatedly to go from the successful extensive accumulation of the first half of its existence to intensive accumulation. The failure showed that it was not a capitalist mode of production, as that by definition is based on intensive accumulation. I analyzed the crisis in terms of social struggles through the resistance of workers, thanks to the right to work and because enterprise directors do not have the legitimacy of a boss in the West, etc. I was saying that an end had come to the social compromise characteristic of the first phase of the system, which allowed extensive accumulation (and underlying this a degree of popular modernization in mass education, broad social mobility, and so on). Palmiro Togliatti, followed by Enrico Berlinguer, have said this too in their way. It was necessary either to go further with the leftist critique of Stalinism or to accelerate rightist evolution toward a normal capitalism or elitist modernization of a third world kind. The bourgeoisie chose the latter: the market—the old story of putting the masses to work through the threat of unemployment; and privatization—to stabilize the bourgeoisie by restricting social mobility, which had emerged as a demand in the later years of the system.

I have always refused to treat the specific crisis in the Soviet mode alongside the totally different crises of capitalism. I have also rejected those analyses of the system offered by the capitalist propaganda machinery and vulgarized in the media.

The distinction between an economy of poverty—i.e., socialism—and an economy of abundance—i.e., capitalism—leads to empty ideological discourse. It is obvious that the poverty shown in long lines, etc. was produced by the voluntary freezing of prices, which permitted broad access to consumer goods—a concession to egalitarian pressures from the masses and the middle strata. It is obvious that if prices rise massively, there are no more lines—but the seemingly vanished poverty is still there, for those who no longer have access to consumer goods. The shops in Mexico and Egypt are packed with goods, and there are no lines in front of the butchers' shops, although meat consumption per head is a third of what it was in Eastern Europe. This childish argument has made a fortune for the Hungarian J. Kornai, promoted by the World Bank.

The command economy, as compared to the self-regulating economy made fashionable by U.S. academics, is also an outrageous simplification. The real Soviet economy was always based on a mixture of adjustments by the market operating outside the plan or foreseen—correctly or not—and administrative orders, especially on investment. The market idealized by the prevailing liberal ideology has never been self-regulating beyond the constraints of the social system where it operates and the state policies that determine its framework. The real problem is that accumulation in the framework of statist centralization of capital (corresponding to an integrated state-class) differs from capitalist accumulation, which in the modern age results not from market laws defined in an ideal abstract but from competition among monopolies.

From as early as 1935 the overall economic apparatus was subject to priority needs in military expenditure. Does this mean that the Soviet system is military? It is suggested by some that it has a natural expansionism through conquest. Similarly, Jean Jaurés had posited that "capitalism bears war within itself like the cloud the storm." I have attacked such ideological nonsense. Analysis of the relative significance, and social burden, of military expenditure cannot be conducted on the grounds purely of modes of production, as its real ground is analysis of the structure and conjuncture of national or local and international or regional global systems. From this viewpoint it is obvious that the arms race was imposed on the USSR by its real enemies and false friends among the capitalist powers.

The discourse on "totalitarianism" lacks coherence. It has pretentious academic forms in the style of Hannah Arendt or childish forms in the media. A U.S. president used the phrase "Evil Empire" to describe its adversary and came close to the kind of language used by Iran's Ayatollah Khomeini. Was it forgotten that a society grown amorphous would never be able to rid itself of despotism?

I saw in Sovietism an attempt to escape the impasse of Stalinism by going to the right rather than the left. The

proposals illustrated what I called "the utopia of construct-
ing a capitalism without capitalists." The Novosibirsk
school, which most influenced Gorbachev, pushed the
logic of Leon Walras to the limit. It imagined a pure and
perfect self-regulating market. As Walras had understood,
and Enrico Barone had been explaining by 1908, this did
not call for dispersed private property but for total statist
centralization of property. It called for the constant bidding
for access to means of production by all individuals who
were free to sell their labor or organize production as
entrepreneurs. The old dream of Saint-Simon of the scientific management of society taken up by German social
democracy (Engels was the first to see it as the dream of
capitalism without capitalists) expresses the economistic
alienation of all bourgeois ideology, whose unreal and
utopian character was shown by historical materialism.

This philosophy is the key to the reformist vision of
Khrushchev and Gorbachev and even the adulterated
version of the Brezhnev period. History has shown that
these concepts were untenable and that the drift to the
right would reach its goal in the transformation of the
Soviet bourgeoisie into a normal private property-owning
bourgeoisie.

The revolution of the years from 1989 to 1991 was
top-down from the ruling class and not bottom-up from
the people. I made a similar observation at the time about
Sadat's counterrevolution of 1971; it was not a counterrevolution but the speeding up of a tendency that was
latent in Nasser's period. The Western media would like to
present the revolutions in the East as blows for freedom;
they neglect to analyze the vulnerability of the
democratization, which may very well be only a means of
ensuring a transition to crude capitalism—always despotic,
as can be seen from the historical experience of the
capitalist peripheries. I disagreed. The revolutions could be
considered blows for freedom only if the system was

overtaken by the left. In their present form they were no more than prodigious and unexpected accelerations of the natural evolution of the system, despite the thesis of totalitarian blockage.

Gorbachev thought he could control the reform process and did not expect to be dumped by the majority of the *nomenklatura* class he represented (as Boris Yeltsin's rise showed), any more than he expected the irrelevance of the Communist Party, which proved to be useless for transmitting the project to the popular level. The Soviet *nomenklatura* bourgeoisie will be the bourgeoisie of tomorrow, directly appropriating the means of production into private hands and no longer collectively through the intermediary of the state. This is not a social revolution but a political upheaval so vast that it requires radical change in the leadership group. (I noted at the time that this was the case in Sadat's counterrevolution.) The parallel rise of a stratum of new rich adventurers (the "mafia" in the USSR) is similar to the so-called parasitic bourgeoisie in Egypt. It was difficult to avoid the sudden political fragmentation of the former *nomenklatura* and the manipulation of the national aspirations of the peoples of the former Soviet Union. This is, of course, the business of the Western powers. They will easily take advantage of the situation through the blackmail of financial aid. They will push the frontiers of Russia back to those of sixteenth-century Muscovy and demolish any hope for the country to be a significant competitor on the world scene.

Here too I offer a self-criticism. I thought—like Gorbachev—that the system was capable of reform and that on this occasion—even though the reform plan was rightist in its vision of economic management—the promising democratic element would enable the popular forces to bend the evolution to the left. I underestimated the disastrous impact of depoliticization which made the working classes vulnerable and unable to make beneficial use of democratization and devise a positive counterplan. Their disarray left them passive and deluded, therefore an easy prey for nationalism. The depoliticization was no less dramatic for the ruling class, tamed by the supreme authority. The ruling class was fragmented into conservatives, Gorbachev supporters, right-wing populists, and so on, and the top-down reform became impossible. I thought the big power nationalism of this class would be a safeguard. I underestimated the ferocious appetite of the candidates for consumerism as they were ready to sacrifice all for the speedy satisfaction of their desire to be rich. I also overestimated the Soviet patriotism of the popular classes, which could not have cared less for the satisfactions a country with the rank of theirs could command. The rejection of patriotism may be healthy in some respects, as in the long term it permits the social project to be brought to the foreground. It is also exceedingly dangerous in the short term, as external adversaries will not fail to exploit it in order to peripheralize Russia and the other nations of the former Soviet Union and turn them into Europe's—especially Germany's—own "Latin America."

For the USSR, as for any other historical society, the external political options were closely linked to the demands of the internal social dynamic. I was never convinced by the ideological thesis that the USSR was intrinsically aggressive or was always peace-loving. I suggested rather a realistic analysis of the way the internal and external dynamics could operate in the USSR, in China, and in the various regions of developed capitalism (United States, Japan, and Europe). I considered various scenarios for the world system and degrees of probability. In this context the correct or distorted projection of reality by the ruling classes cannot be ignored. This is true of all authorities in office, Soviet or other.

Obviously there is no guarantee of the correctness of a realistic analysis. It is influenced by passing events and may be extrapolated in a way that is subsequently disproved. I shall give some examples that provide a motive for self-criticism.

An analysis of the USSR's external policies and their assessment from a humanist, democratic, and socialist outlook on a world scale must explicitly refer to the world system in which the policies under criticism were implemented.

Until the 1960s the Soviet system was fairly isolated and on the defensive. The view I took at the time still seems correct—even with hindsight. I put forward several positions that I shall only summarize here.

Not for a moment since 1917 have the fascist and democratic Western powers abandoned the idea of defeating the Soviet Union. Despite the USSR's decisive role in defeating the Axis powers, it emerged exhausted from World War II and was threatened by the United States's nuclear monopoly. The Yalta agreements were not a division of the world between victorious imperialisms but a minimum guarantee the Soviet Union had won for its own security.

The Soviet Union, like China, Vietnam, or Cuba, has never sought to export revolution but has on the contrary always practiced prudent diplomacy, with the primary purpose of defending its own state. All the revolutions were conducted virtually against the will of Big Brother: China against the advice of Moscow, and Vietnam and Cuba acting on their own. This fact never shocked me, and I tried to fathom the reasons, without accepting that revolutionaries must submit to it. They should rather go further and be self-reliant. Successful revolutionaries have done this (China, Vietnam, Cuba, Kampuchea, Nicaragua).

The Cold War was Washington's initiative after 1947. The USSR stuck rigidly to the division at Yalta (hence its attitude to the revolution in Greece) and never in its history did it nurture a project to invade Western Europe. Talk of Soviet bellicosity is pure Western propaganda. The Zhdanov doctrine of a world divided into two camps was characteristically defensive (justifying the nonintervention of the USSR beyond the Yalta boundaries) and inaugurated a period of Western isolation of the USSR, and of China after 1949. The Atlantic powers never once ceased interfering in the third world with colonial wars, Israeli aggression, and so on.

The USSR and China began to leave their isolation after the 1955 Bandung conference, when they saw the advantage they could gain from giving support, albeit limited, to third world liberation movements. I have never blamed them for this historically useful support, and I never expected more than could be given during the search for peaceful coexistence refused by the Atlantic bloc.

The belated Soviet military effort after about 1970 contributed to a genuine balance of deterrence. Then, but only then, did the USSR become a superpower and a new era begin.

The bipolarity characteristic of the twenty years before the Soviet collapse of 1989-1991 is asymmetrical in that the USSR was a superpower only in military terms without being able to compete with the Western imperialists in their capacity for economic intervention.

There was never a symmetry between the actions of the two superpowers and their impact. The United States, with Europe and Japan in the background, pursued a diplomacy of clear goals and familiar methods: to ensure domination of the periphery (access to raw materials, markets, military bases, etc.). The United States established hegemony through this shared strategy and when U.S. economic advantage over its allies began to erode, it used the strategy to maintain its declining hegemony (the Gulf War is the most recent episode).

The goals of Soviet intervention beyond the Yalta boundaries are more difficult to identify. I have argued that the main goal was to loosen the Western stranglehold, or to breach the Atlantic alliance by separating Europe from the United States. They did so mainly through support of third world liberation movements and national radical governments (Palestine and the Arab world, the Horn of Africa, Angola and Mozambique, the "African socialist" states). Europe was reminded of its vulnerability and dependence on oil supplies and encouraged to distance itself from the United States and to negotiate. The strategic aim was not to weaken Europe and invade but to bring it to active peaceful coexistence capable of supporting the USSR's economic development, a development moving to the right. De Gaulle was the only European political leader to understand—and accept—this approach. The Soviet scheme failed, and neither Khrushchev's carrot nor Brezhnev's stick produced the desired result, any more than the renewed carrot from Gorbachev and Yeltsin persuaded the Europeans to abandon their own agenda of weakening the USSR as much as possible and encouraging its break-up.

Soviet support of third world peoples and governments was naturally limited. I have always been sympathetic to this without ever underwriting its theoretical legitimations such as the "noncapitalist road," which I have criticized on occasion as damaging to the success of third world progressive forces. I was, of course, vilified by the sycophants of the Moscow Academy, including some who now head the roll of anticommunists, and the unconditional supporters of the USSR in Africa, the Middle East, Cuba, and Vietnam.

I did not see Soviet interventions as an aggressive determination to export revolution and to dominate, but rather as a defensive posture from comparative weakness despite the acquisition of parity in nuclear deterrence.

The interventions have sometimes been perceived as a manifestation of growing strength. This requires consideration of the debate on "social imperialism," a term devised by the Chinese in 1963. It was a plan for a social compromise between the Soviet bourgeoisie and its people—a revisionist compromise. It was after all similar to the social-democratic compromise in the West and would have allowed external expansion similar to the colonial expansion supported by the imperialist consensus in the West. There was nothing startling or unimaginable in the concept. The real issue was not whether the Soviet bourgeoisie did or did not want to embark on it but whether it was capable of it. I think the answer to this remains open.

There were clear signs that at least some Soviet authorities dreamed of following this path. In the 1960s a plan of aggression against China was initiated, with the overt goal of dismembering China and dividing it between the USSR, Japan, and the Western powers.[1]

I make no self-criticism of what I wrote at the time consistent with the hypothesis of social imperialism. Moscow backed off a few years later.

Brezhnev's regime continued to look strong from the outside and was so judged in most anti-socialist analyses of the time. I had my own reservations on this apparent strength and found in this the explanation for Brezhnev's abandonment of an aggressive attitude to China. I voiced the fear that the regime might trip up, as the useless invasion of Afghanistan hinted, and was relying increasingly on military strength rather than persuading the world of its socialist beliefs. It made concessions that suggested economic difficulties and the relatively limited success of the rightist line it adopted to overcome them.

I have pointed to the limitations and risks of various analyses from 1970 to 1990 of the possible scenarios for the evolution of the world system. Such analysis has its merits as it demands an explanation of what is too often left unexplained in analyses not carried to a logical conclusion. I shall pass by the various debates in which I participated. Some of the debates are finished. There is no mileage now in the notion of a global scenario strengthening Soviet social imperialism on a world scale by taking advantage of U.S. decline and bringing together the Soviet's revisionist compromise and a broadly similar compromise within a Europe of the left. That may never have been more than a joke. I did take it seriously for a while. I made the mistake of underestimating the internal weaknesses of the Soviet system and overestimating the European left.

The debate is on-going on a broad realignment of international alliances, a Paris-Bonn-Moscow axis, a Washington-Tokyo-Beijing axis, etc. The realignment could lead to a European Atlantic role, a wider gap between the United States and Europe, a European shift to the left. The arguments remain valid, although the probability of a particular scenario rises or falls. I raised four issues that remain central even now after the collapse of the Soviet system.

Can the integration of the East in the world system be a significant element in the outcome of the crisis of world capitalism, now that "socialism" no longer exists? The question raised more than five years ago is even more pertinent now, although the answer I gave seems to me to have been contradicted by events in the short term. I said then that the bourgeois Soviet Union would control its integration into world capitalism.

Is it feasible to reconstitute an integrated world market? This question too dates back more than five years and remains current. This is regardless of whether the Soviet Union, when integrated into the market, would occupy its place as a new capitalist center or as a new industrialized periphery. I maintain my principled stand that the idea of reconstituting the integrated world market is utopian.[2]

Are state and nation active subjects of history in the way that class is? This question arises from the weakening of serious social struggles in the components of the modern world to the immediate benefit of the rivalry and conflict between existing states or those emerging from the disintegration of multinational states. This is the familiar debate dating from the 1960s based on the Chinese theory of three worlds: "states seek independence, nations liberation, and peoples revolution." I shall say no more except that I do not find what I wrote at the time contradicted by current events—indeed, much the reverse. My thesis on chaos picks up this discussion and carries it into the circumstances of our time.

Are changes leading toward a Eurasian bloc of Europe and the USSR in De Gaulle's terms or toward Gorbachev's plan for a "common house"? Has this nightmare prospect for the United States been avoided by Europe's vacillating policies, internal contradictions, the Atlantic alliance, and the coming together of Moscow and Washington? I believe the immediate result has provided a second wind for U.S. hegemony, eclipsing Europe again to the benefit of the United States's shining seconds, Japan and Germany.[3]

The collapse of the Soviet system, although it has been predictable for a long time, is a major event of our time. All scenarios for the future must take the new circumstances into account.

Does the collapse mean an end to socialism and Marxism, as the major media like to say, the "end of history," the triumph of a monolithic consensus ensuring the perpetual survival of the capitalist ethos? I believe this is nonsense, even though an era is obviously ending.

The era of Socialism I established in the nineteenth century, ended in 1914 with the failure of the social-democratic parties of the Second International, which became overt accomplices in their national imperialisms. Lenin was right to declare Socialism I dead at that moment.

Its successor, Socialism II, of the Third International and Leninism, is now dead after a long illness. Since 1963 I have been writing that the advance of socialism required a rupture with Sovietism as radical as that made by Lenin in 1914. It is also significant that the Soviet system, in its overt recruitment to capitalism, takes the same position as that prevailing in Western culture against the third world, namely against three-quarters of humankind.

The death of a child does not bring the parent back to life. The grandchild must carry on the task of the ancestors. Long live Socialism III to come.

Are the outlines of this Socialism-to-come already visible? I believe they are, and I have the temerity to put forward the three lessons I have learned in the past thirty years in my dual critique of the Soviet system and capitalist globalization:

(1). Creating an alternative must come before catching up at all costs.

(2). World polarization implies that delinking is the only choice, even if the means must constantly be reviewed in light of the constraints of general evolution.

(3). Systematic action must be undertaken to rebuild a polycentric world, thus providing scope for the people's autonomous progress.

These three conditions determine a potential and necessary renaissance for an internationalism of all the people on the earth able to combat the internationalism of capital. It offers a prospect, albeit distant, of a socialism that can only be worldwide and able to meet the challenge of globalization or rapidly decline and perish.

A decade ago I suggested opening a debate on the transition beyond capitalism. I took a long look at history free of the scholastic distinction between reform or revolution, and I suggested that there were two forms of transition. One I described as revolutionary, although possible through a range of consistent reforms; it entailed a certain ideological consciousness capable of expressing the demands of a new social project. This was the passage to capitalism. The other implied no ideological consciousness. The objective constraints determined events. This one was decadent, since it implied the anarchic break-up of the old system. An example was the passage to European feudalism.

The tributary centralization of the Roman Empire became an obstacle to the advance of the barbarian peoples. Advancement demanded fragmentation of the centralization represented by feudalism on the basis of which was reconstructed much later a new centralization of surplus achieved by capitalism. In the same way today's centralization of surplus by capitalism on a world scale has become an obstacle to the advance of three-quarters of humankind. The rebuilding of a unified world system going beyond capitalist polarization requires, therefore, a break-up of the system of capitalist centralization of surplus. It requires delinking.

Will humankind be able to control this transition to some degree? It can do so only through the renaissance of a serious worldwide movement of Socialism III. In the alternative the objective constraints will allow the long decadence of society, through redoubled violence of senseless conflicts, or barbarism. In an age such as ours—when there are enough weapons to destroy the whole earth, when the media can tame the crowds with frightening efficiency, when short-term egoism or anti-humanist individualism is a fundamental value threatening earth's ecological survival—barbarism may be fatal.

More than ever the choice we face is not capitalism or socialism, but socialism or barbarism.

8

The System in Crisis: The Collapse of Capitalist Regulatory Mechanisms

Capitalism, like any living system, is based on contradictions that it ceaselessly overcomes without being demolished. The shaping of social forces, the machinery, and the institutions that enable capitalism to overcome some contradictions constitute at any given time what might be described as its regulatory mode. As soon as the capacity of the system to overcome its contradictions is acknowledged, the question arises: how long will this last? It is a vital question for anyone who identifies with the victims of the system and wants to contribute to identifying the strategies of struggle against capitalism.

First, we need to identify the genuine contradictions of actually existing capitalism and their interaction. We should not assume that the system has presented the same underlying structure to these contradictions throughout its history. It is important to observe the qualitatively different phases through which the structure, and by implication its regulatory system, has passed. The regulation approach has certainly helped to bring out the specific character of Fordist capitalism, but this approach has seemed limited and inadequate to me because entire aspects of capitalism other than Fordism went unexamined. In other words, it focused on the advanced centers of capitalism and forgot that actually existing capitalism is a world system. The advanced centers are not the image of what the periphery will be tomorrow, but the periphery cannot be understood outside its relation to the world system as a whole.[1]

I shall not repeat the history of successive phases of capitalism until it took its full shape with the Industrial Revolution or suggest the various kinds of regulation practiced during this history. Such an exercise would not help distinguish what was or was not regulated, or what precise national or worldwide contradictions were or were not overcome at a particular period. I shall say only that the attenuation of some contradictions through a regulatory system shifts the conflict to other contradictions, which then come into play with redoubled force. This observation is relevant to anyone interested in effective strategies of struggle against capitalism.

The capitalist mode of production is defined by an essential contradiction between capital and labor in the precise meaning Marx gave these terms. The labor is that of a free individual obliged to dispose of his or her labor power as his or her sole wealth. Capital is the social relationship that allows a particular social class, the bourgeoisie, to appropriate the accumulated surplus labor of the past in those means of production without which modern production is unimaginable. This commonplace must be remembered at a time when an increasing confusion of concepts equates capital with wealth, capital accumulation with monetary accumulation, capitalism with exchange, and destroys the significance of the qualitative transformations brought by the capitalist mode of production.[2]

I am not saying that this is the sole or principal contradiction underlying the driving conflicts of evolution and change. I am saying merely that the essential contradiction of the capitalist mode of production makes the system continually tend to overproduce. This phenomenon is unknown in history before the Industrial Revolution.

It is easy to illustrate this fact.[3] In a model of extended production reduced to Marx's Departments I and II, the realization of surplus value requires from one period to another a growth in real wages that is mathematically linked to that of the productivity of labor. The social relationship between bourgeoisie and proletariat operates against this necessary adjustment. Wages tend to be below what might be expected from productivity. The system spontaneously generates a tendency to overproduction, or underconsumption, as the two are opposite sides of the same phenomenon: the proletariat does not earn enough money to buy the goods that it produces.

Stagnation is not the problem, as the eulogistic ideological language of capitalism suggests. It is its opposite: prodigious growth achieved by the system despite the inherent tendency to stagnation. I have suggested a position on Kondratieff long cycles consistent with Baran and Sweezy's analysis and in contrast to fashionable thinking on the subject.[4] I argue that each expansionary phase is matched by major innovations and political regulation to expand markets. I cite the first Industrial Revolution, the railway, electricity, postwar reconstruction, and the Cold War. For the future we have the reconquest of Eastern Europe and the former USSR, and the information and space age.

The inherent tendency to stagnation has required the developed capitalist centers to develop a Department III to absorb the surplus in luxury consumption (I adopt Baran and Sweezy's argument) as an essential regulatory lever. The United States could overcome the crisis of the 1930s only through huge military expenditures on World War II and the subsequent Cold War.

This political regulation is available only to central capitalist states. On a world scale there is a lack of regulation, which becomes a deployment of the effect of the law of accumulation (or immiseration). Marx underestimated worldwide polarization and incorrectly generalized this law to each of the national subsystems comprising the world capitalist economy. It is observable only on a global scale, because if income distribution tends to be stable in the centers, social inequality increases with development in the peripheries.[5]

The Industrial Revolution from 1800 to 1920, the first long phase of capitalism, was the period of mechanized industry studied by Marx in *Capital.* The system during this period reproduced itself on an ever expanding base, both vertically in labor productivity and horizontally in geographical spread. This means that it overcame contradictions and can be examined in terms of regulation.

It may help to understand what was regulated and what contradictions were reduced if we briefly recall the apparent characteristics of the system at this time. This was a period when national capitalist productive systems that were industrial and autocentric were constructed. They were built within a framework of active intervention by the new bourgeois nation state.

The national economic structure had particular characteristics. Small and medium-sized mechanized industrial plants had a competitive advantage over the former artisans and had an expanding market in the enriched bourgeoisie and new working class. On the other hand, agriculture and services were scarcely modernized, and operated within a market framework that was barely capitalist. The market for savings and finance was organized through highly personalized regional networks of small banks and lawyers supplying family capitalist businesspeople. The national market was increasingly integrated in three aspects: a market for new industrial products and the peasants' surplus crop, a market for capital through the interconnection of regional networks, and an industrial labor market through urbanization and internal migration from the rural areas.

The social system was dominated by a bourgeoisie of family industrialists, financiers, and rural and urban property owners. Factory labor drew on skilled workers who had mastered the manufacturing process, often recruited from the ruined former artisans and the few engineers to be found at this stage of technological development. Unskilled laborers doing heavy work were recruited from the impoverished peasants driven from the countryside. Pressure from the surplus rural population was relieved by emigration to the Americas. This contributed to the acceleration of American development.

I see two regulatory systems at the national level—a system of political alliances and a system of centralized management of money and credit—but no regulatory system at the international level.

The national regulatory system is essentially political in character. Capital had to isolate the restless new working class concentrated in the towns (in the military control techniques of the time, the barricade served its purpose). The bourgeoisie reached compromises according to their historical circumstances, with the peasants (mostly middle peasants after the radical revolution in France) or with the aristocracy (in England and Prussia, and later on in Germany). Economic methods used in the anti-worker bourgeois hegemonic alliance included protection for domestic agricultural markets, agricultural credit to protect the small and medium-sized landowner, and distortion of the tax base in favor of peasants or aristocratic owners. The alliance was manifest in a peasant living standard higher than that of the working class. Regulation also incorporated social and political practices: limited suffrage (universal suffrage was a late arrival), elite and stratified education, the division of political duties, with special rights for the English aristocracy, the German emperor, etc.

Regulation generally operated against capital accumulation, so that it was slower than predicted by an abstract model of the relationship between capital and labor.

The economic regulatory system at this stage was based on national control of money and credit; this played an important role which is usually underestimated or ignored.[6]

Credit is essential for extended reproduction. To show this I used a Marxian model of Departments I and II. According to the hypothesis that the issue of realization is resolved by a growth in real wages mathematically linked to the productivity of labor, realization of the product demands the injection of a defined volume of credit advanced to capitalists at the start of each cycle and repaid by them at the end, and the volume is also subject to the constraint of a defined growth mathematically linked to product expansion through a growth in productivity. Here one recognizes the problem Rosa Luxemburg met (that of the realization of the product), and to which I think she gave the wrong answer. Lenin, on the other hand, avoided the difficulty. My answer recognized what I called the active role of credit in capitalist accumulation as a complement to its passive role, acknowledged in classical Marxism as the adjustment of the supply of money to demand.

Bourgeois ideology offered in this field, as in others, a spuriously scientific and tautologous analysis: the supply and demand of credit spontaneously achieve the necessary equilibrium. I showed, on the contrary, that the credit market accentuated the cyclical fluctuations. I argued the case at two moments. In the first, a model of the cycle was developed without consideration of credit, operating solely through the play of the multiplier linking investment to final demand, with the accelerator operating in the reverse way (i.e., linking final demand to investment). The model showed that the extended reproduction of the pre-Fordist, pre-Keynesian era took on a natural-looking cyclical form, produced by the operation of the specific contradictions of capitalism being regularly overcome and then reappearing. Then, introducing credit, I showed that the laws of the relevant market played a role of amplifying, not smoothing out, the real cycle.[7]

No regulation operates at the international level, whether in the economic management of relations between central capitalist states or in their political relations.

The most common thesis in this field is that the gold or sterling standard associated with British hegemony is a regulatory system constraining national policies, which are therefore obliged to react appropriately to the signals of the external balance of payments, in a system largely open to commercial flows limited only by customs tariffs and to capital movements that are in principle always free.

Here I return to my arguments on the supposedly spontaneous readjustment of the external balance.[8] I examined the logical validity of economic theories about this and the mechanics of this operation under the gold standard or in a system of flexible currency rates detached from gold. I rejected the idea of spontaneous readjustment. It seemed to me that these theories of price, exchange, and income effects failed to prove that markets achieved equilibrium except by presupposing what they endeavored to prove. They were therefore empty tautology. I accused this economic theory of being "bound up with the ideology of universal harmony." I concluded that no international regulation was possible, as it would imply interconnecting national development policies—a kind of "world planning" that is in contradiction with the very idea of international competition. The crude equilibrium was achieved only through constant structural adjustment (the very words I used), nothing more than the adjustment of the weakest to the constraints of accumulation by the strongest. This takes us from the realm of economics to the realm of politics.

The real operation of international politics is unregulated. Here once again, the most common thesis is that British hegemony ensured this regulation, as U.S. hegemony does nowadays—or failing that, the shared hegemony of the G-7 (or the G-3—the United States, Japan, and Germany). I have strong reservations about theses of political regulation based on a theory of hegemony that is too broad and taken too far back in time.

As might be expected, it is fashionable to talk of hegemony nowadays. According to the liberal American Robert Keohane, hegemony secures stability by imposing respect for the rules of the game. I have a quite different analysis of the New World Order heralded by the United States in the Gulf War and coming immediately and not coincidentally in the wake of Soviet disintegration. I analyze it in terms of a new "empire of chaos," one of maximum instability beset with violent contradictions: renewed rivalry between the centers and explosions in the periphery of the South and the East. Political regulation is not on the agenda.[9]

By contrast, throughout this phase management of economic and political relations between the capitalist centers and the peripheries was comparatively easy. The peripheries were maintained as nonindustrialized regions through direct colonization and foreign administration, with British policy in India a typical example. Contrary to the common misconception, integration into the world capitalist system did not create a local bourgeoisie but tended rather to destroy it in the embryo.[10] These regions were also kept nonindustrialized through the system of political alliances of dominant imperialism, British especially, with local reactionary classes, *latifundia* property in Latin America, and Chinese, Ottoman, Khedival, or Persian imperial power. Local authorities accepted integration in the world system and an open door to trade, sometimes at gunpoint, and the ruling classes benefitted by becoming comprador commodity producers. Britain as a hegemonic power owed its hegemony more to these overseas relations than to any capacity to manage advantageously the inter-center relations, and a European balance was largely outside its grasp. I describe these relations as imperialist, since imperialism to me means using political means for unequal capitalist expansion and shaping the center-periphery relationship. In this sense imperialism is not a new phase of capitalism linked directly to the construction of the monopolies, but a constant feature of capitalism. Imperialism must always be seen in the plural: the centers create their own peripheral reserves, or try to do so, and are in continual conflict on the ground.

In international relations the states of the periphery not under formal colonization were not recognized as enjoying full rights or genuine sovereignty. They were treated as space available for world capitalist expansion. The system of sovereign states remained European from the Treaty of Westphalia in 1648 to the Congress of Vienna in 1815 to the Treaty of Versailles in 1919. It was complemented by the Monroe Doctrine's parallel system of American states—the North American center and the Latin American periphery. The state system was not made universal until the UN Charter in 1945.

Center-periphery relations were a significant factor in the extended capitalist reproduction that continued until after World War II, when the national liberation movements won their independence and forced accompanying internal social changes. The peripheries supplied raw materials and agricultural cash crops on terms of unequal exchange (a price differential above that of the differential of productivities). This raised the rate of profit at the center by reducing its component costs, whether fixed capital (raw materials) or variable capital (wage goods).

This analysis shows that regulatory systems do not operate exclusively on production relations, in the domain of political economy, but influence social relations. The latter are broader than the production relations, and as they involve the state, social power, and ideology, they belong to the broader domain of historical materialism.

More generally, it may be observed that the state's role in the forms of regulation was both complementary and

contradictory. The state created conditions for reproduction of the fundamental production relations for the pursuit of a historical form of class domination, namely
capitalism in its national and worldwide aspects. The state
also created conditions for the reproduction of social
relations guaranteeing the general interest, namely
transcending conflicting social interests. This was manifest
in what was conventionally called the "national interest."
Its content was the historic compromise between capital
and peasants or capital and the aristocracy. In the later
Fordist phase, the historic compromise between capital and
labor brought in the social-democratic welfare states of the
advanced West. In order to reconcile the roles, the state
became autonomous . The state developed its own logic of
power which clashed with the logic of accumulation,
partially in the center and seriously in the periphery, where
it was impossible to reconcile national interest with the
constraint of globalization.

Our understanding of regulatory mechanisms is handicapped by the limitations actually existing Marxism has
imposed on itself. Marx hoped to lay the groundwork for
a historical materialism that would account for the
economics of capitalism, state, power, culture, and ideology.
He outlined the foundations in his writings. Unhappily, in
the aftermath, instead of a pursuit of historical materialism
emerged what is called "Marxism" and is more an inventory
and vulgarization of Marx's own discoveries and propositions. The dogmatism was not an invention of Stalin. It dates
back to the old German social democracy of the late
nineteenth century, whose concepts were largely inherited
by what became Leninism, then its Stalinist descendant
(and even its rival, Trotskyism), and in part Maoism, possibly the most open current of historical Marxism. At a
stroke the theories of power and ideology were truncated
or reduced to pallid and pointless pseudo-theory as compared to the theory of the capitalist mode of production.

The regulation approach was taken to advance a realistic analysis of capitalism in its later phase, described as Fordist by the regulation theorists themselves. The particular form of this new phase, which began in the United States around 1920, did not spread to Europe and Japan until after 1945 and faded out in the crisis of 1968. The period broadly covers the half-century from 1920 to 1970.

The breakthrough was prepared by Harry Braverman's remarkable work on the changes in the labor process caused by assembly-line production.[11] Braverman, as meticulous as Marx had been in his study of labor in the mechanized industry of his time, put his finger on the essentials. The new system entailed a massive deskilling of labor. It replaced the former skilled working class with a laboring mass. The new working class lost control over the labor process to the benefit of administrators and organizers. Control passed to the slave drivers at the workplace.

The new organization of capital and labor also created the conditions for a new regulatory system, which became objectively necessary as capitalism's spontaneous tendency to overproduce was exacerbated. Labor productivity, substantially raised by Frederick Taylor's "scientific management," would have generated an unabsorbable excess production if real wages had remained comparatively stable. The new laboring mass, which was more homogeneous than in the previous stage, was receptive to the spread of trade unionism. The old forms of competition were centered exclusively on price and this put pressure on wages. The concentration of capital and the rise of oligopolies brought new forms of competition based on improved productivity requiring a measure of cooperation from the workers and a multiplication and differentiation of products. The scene was set for the employers and the unions to agree on an income policy acceptable to both sides. The antagonistic classes began to be spoken of as social partners. The state entered the stage to ensure that the policies negotiated by the strongest and best-organized partners should be extended to all labor relations in the nation.

The essence of this new wage policy was simply to link the rise in real wages to the rise in productivity. The state provided the framework to link progress in average wages (the minimum wage, which was the effective wage for the majority) to progress in average productivity on a national scale. Sector and plant-level negotiators geared their own agreements to the nationally defined norm.

That is all the new regulation is. The significant contribution of the regulation approach was not only to explain it but also to link its implementation to the emergence of the social-democratic welfare state.

The new regulation smoothed out the average seven-year cycles so characteristic of the previous phase, as it lessened the impact of the accelerator (investment levels varying with output and final demand). It brought an element of investment planning free from speculation. State intervention could now be gentler, less jarring, but more rapidly responsive by adjusting public expenditure and borrowing requirements, tax levies, and so on. Credit regulation was also reduced as credit became subject to the more embracing logic.

The new regulation did not prevent the tendency of the system to overproduction. Keynes had the wit to understand this. The state reappeared to promote a Department III to absorb the surplus through luxury consumption (by analogy with the Marxian model of extended reproduction and Departments I and II—capital goods and consumer goods). We owe to Baran and Sweezy this reformulation of the system of extended production.[12] Unfortunately, there is widespread refusal to accept that this aspect of control of reproduction is no less important than that arising from wage policy. I see no other explanation than the notorious prejudice about overproduction, a prejudice engendered by vulgar Marxism and the dogmatic readings of Marx it has inspired.

It is impossible to understand all aspects of regulation without considering the social and ideological effects of mass production methods. The social compromise entailed changing attitudes in the working class, abandonment of the dream of a socialist society based on the abolition of private property, and adherence to a new ideology of mass consumption. The working class ceased to be what Marx expected: the liberator of society from economistic alienation. For the first time, bourgeois ideology really became the dominant ideology in society. Bourgeois ideology was based on a separation of the realm of politics and the realm of economics. Politics was managed by the bourgeois democracy and dealt with freedoms and multiparty elections. Economics was managed nondemocratically on the basis of private property, competition, and the laws of the market. The new regulation portended an erosion of democracy. The dual consensus of political democracy and market laws lessened the impact of the old distinction between right and left, conservatism and dynamism, the moneyed classes and the popular classes. It allowed the spread of the middle classes into a leading role in the ideological shaping of society. It created the model of the average citizen determining modes of communication, social aspiration, etc.

Regulation was strictly national. It was constructed within autocentric productive systems still largely autonomous, notwithstanding their interdependence within a world market. It worked only to the degree that the national state exercised effective control over its means of managing the national economy and its external exchanges in trading competitiveness, capital, and technology flows. This could apply only to the central capitalist states. It must again be stressed that regulation was effective only for the countries high up in the world hierarchy. In the weaker, comparatively less centrally developed capitalist societies, the difficulties of reconciling the internal social compromise and the constraints of international competition could be seen in repeated and serious crises in which the reform endeavor was often stymied.

On a world scale, regulation at the center implies reproduction of the unequal center-periphery relationship. This aspect is sadly ignored by all those who take the conventional view of separating "development" dependent on internal factors peculiar to each society from reproduction of the world system, or what I have termed the polarization inherent in the worldwide expansion of capitalism. The arguments are familiar: The peripheries do not provide an essential market for exports from the center or for investment capital. The centers can do without the raw materials from the peripheries. This I believe is superficial nonsense. Actually existing capitalism cannot do without access to the whole earth's riches, of which the centers consume or waste more than three-quarters. Ecology has recently rediscovered this commonplace evidence. The most dynamic central capitalist powers benefit from all kinds of monopolies on a world scale. They accumulate and centralize capital, and contrary to developmentalist discourse, the peripheries are usually net exporters of capital to the centers. These centers accentuate their benefit from technological advance through the brain drain. Privileged access to the peripheries is a significant component of competition between the centers.[13] But the Fordist period from 1920 to 1970 coincided with the rise, after 1945, of the national liberation movements that brought Asian and African independence. This changed the circumstances of international competition and heightened strategic considerations. The United States was first able to profit from Cold War "anticommunism" and then, as soon as the USSR was in the final throes of break-up, to substitute a common front of North against South (witness the Gulf War). This demonstrated the crucial importance of the world factor against all the economistic discourse about so-called marginalization of the third world.

From within the advanced capitalist societies, Fordist regulation may favorably be described as "social democratic." From the viewpoint of a world which is three-quarters periphery, the regulation may less favorably be described as "social imperialist."[14]

The regulatory system of the Fordist period is questionable and, in my view, has no future. It is nowadays very difficult to imagine even a partial alternative regulatory system as long as the outcome of current confrontations is unknown. The contradictions of tomorrow's world will depend on what happens in the immediate future to the current confrontations.

Most regulation theorists explain the crisis through the evolution of workers' struggles at the center. The laboring masses developed methods of passive resistance that canceled the organizational efforts to improve labor productivity. The margin of profit shrank and capitalism lost its suppleness. The argument is, I believe, correct. It must, however, be seen with other factors bringing an end to Fordist regulation.

The Fordist forms of the labor process are in decline. The technological revolution is quickly bringing in new forms of production. Productivity gains that can be made in sectors of Fordist production are limited. The market for goods produced in the Fordist manner is virtually saturated in the centers. The new technologies offer broad scope for productivity to advance through computerization and robotics. This brings a reduced role for social democracy for the Fordist workers. They are the unskilled but unionized mass laborers whose numbers are falling relatively and sometimes absolutely. People like to say that a new skilled labor is being promoted. This is true, but the reskilling is occurring in a society dominated by the middle classes, which reinforces their number and their status by eroding the old forms of democratic political management of society. This factor brings a wide margin of uncertainty into political behavior and therefore into the outcome of national and international confrontations. The uncertainty appears in the "incoherence" or "irrationality" of the actions and reactions of political players on the contemporary scene to an extent unthinkable just a few years ago. The right-wing vote, often at the popular level, in the West, East, and South is genuinely disturbing and must be taken seriously.

The new technological revolution is less capital intensive than the former major revolutions (the railway, electrification, the automobile, urbanization). Technology intensifies the immediate disequilibrium between the supply of available savings (generated within a particular national and world structure of income distribution) and the demand for productive investment (with the expanding technological revolution governing progress in productivity). Thus exacerbated, capitalism's tendency to overproduce was further exacerbated by financial globalization leading to a massive capital transfer from the peripheries to the centers (with debt as one method of such transfer). Sweezy and Magdoff were, I believe, right to stress the system's reaction in a flight toward speculation.[15] Paul Boccara drew attention to capital's systematic devaluation process in its attempt to deal with the disequilibrium: management of permanent inflation, public sector expenditure, etc.[16] All these policies can be classified as regulation since they are short- and medium-term methods of managing a disequilibrium that would in their absence become explosive.

The regulatory system of the Fordist period is also in fatal decline because of increasing interpenetration of national productive systems at the center and the shift from an international economy to a world economy for the first time in history, as Michel Beaud was right to argue.[17] This interpenetration destroys the effectiveness of traditional national policies and delivers the overall system to the dictates and errors of the constraint of the world market, which cannot be regulated as there are no genuinely supranational political institutions, or even a political and social consciousness that really accepts this new demand of capitalism.

This new contradiction is not in my view susceptible to regulation. It can only spread chaos. Considering what I said earlier about the erosion of democratic political systems, the chaos is dangerous. I believed it helpful to highlight these serious problems, the uncertainties that burden the future of EEC Europe (in contrast to the euphoria on the ground), the imbalances between the United States, Japan, and Europe characteristic of the new world system, and the no less serious uncertainties introduced by the change in Eastern Europe and Russia.[18] My intuitive feeling is that the national factor is far from neutralized by the change imposed by the economic system. Quite the reverse: it is making itself felt anew against the very logic of economic change.

A new regulatory system is also unlikely because of the future of center-periphery relations, between West and South and, increasingly, between West and the former East.

The increasing globalization of the structural crisis that developed in the 1970s enabled some countries on the periphery to make their mark as industrial exporters competing with the most vulnerable of the central capitalist economies. Some people rushed to bury the concept of worldwide polarization. This new industrialization is based on the deployment of Fordism without a social-democratic compromise. It is based on a crude capitalism that is, to me, a sure sign of the constitution of the true periphery of tomorrow. This is a kind of industrial putting-out work controlled by the technological and financial monopolies of the dominant centers; it requires an authoritarian state. The Asian and Latin American countries on this path are now joined by Eastern Europe and Russia. At the same time, this "rise" of new peripheral forms disadvantages the medium powers in all of EEC Europe except Germany, to the benefit of the United States and Japan.

The real question is whether the expansion of peripheral industrialization will come within a global system that inevitably accepts the rules of the game that the newly increased globalization enjoins.

Giovanni Arrighi has given an affirmative answer. He has argued that globalization restored communication between the proletariat's active and passive reserve armies, who became separated during the long period of break-up of the world system illustrated by Soviet delinking from 1917 to 1991. I have reservations on this point.[19] Arrighi argues that, according to Marx, capital accumulation would have two complementary effects: (1) strengthening the social power of the active army in the organized industrial working class, and (2) pauperizing the passive reserve army of the unemployed—marginalized workers in precapitalist or low-productivity sectors. In my view, historical Marxism did not notice the geographical and political separation of the active and passive reserve armies in the center and periphery and the significance of worldwide polarization. Historical Marxism supposed that the constant toing and froing of individual proletarians between the two armies would ensure unity on the anticapitalist front and speedy success in its global action. Polarization explains the opposite of a broken unity and two contrasting anticapitalist strategies. The working classes of the centers pursue a social-democratic strategy. The passive army on a world scale is concentrated among the peoples of the periphery, who therefore pursue a Leninist-Maoist revolutionary strategy. Marx had a political vision of regulation through class struggle on a world scale. The vision remains correct and fundamental, although the struggle operates in ways other than Marx expected.

One wonders if the gradual industrialization of the peripheries and the reintegration into the system of the Eastern countries is restoring Marx's dictum: "Workers of the world, unite!" I do not think so because the new polarization will be reproduced as long as the world capitalist market does not allow the constitution of an integrated world labor market. This will continue to bring violent reactions from the peoples in the peripheries. The peoples and the ruling classes of the new industrialized world, and of the fourth world in the East and South, have not yet had their last word. My feeling is that their next round of revolt will challenge the expected globalization. The national state will have its revenge. I do not see how, in a situation of acute conflict between centers and peripheries and in center against center, any regulatory mode can match the scale of problems that arise. Rather, I see the future more as mounting chaos.

A Note on Historical Materialism

My thesis that polarization was inherent in capitalism obliged me to rethink some of the propositions of historical Marxism. I had also always wondered why capitalism appeared in Europe and not in one of the Eastern regions more advanced in previous centuries and even millennia. An answer to this question, I thought, could illuminate the present Third World and indicate the way to change it.

In this chapter I shall retrace the steps in the formulation of some of my general propositions derived from my analysis of the theory of accumulation and polarization and my critiques of development concepts and practices. Some of the propositions deal with the past, precapitalist formations and transition to capitalism, and some with the present, the specific character of capitalism, the nation, the cultural aspect, and the socialist challenge.

THE SPECIFIC CHARACTER OF CAPITALISM

These are the key points of the conception of the specific character of capitalism, from which I have never strayed.

(1). The capitalist mode of production is the first social system based on generalized value: all social production as well as labor and access to resources tend to become commodities.

(2). Value determines not only the economics of capitalism but all forms of social life operating within it.

(3). The dominance of value frees economic laws from their previous subjection to the logic of power. These laws acquire an autonomy such that they are imposed on society like laws of nature. Capitalism is the first social system governed by economic dominance whose realm becomes a possible subject for scientific study.

(4). The economic laws expressed in the generalized law of value mystify the social relations on which they are based, notably exploitation of the labor force. This mystification gives the ideology of capitalism its peculiar character as an ideology of alienated commodities.

(5). The dominance of the economic base implies a particular relation between the economic and the political and ideological instances of social life. It creates the conditions for a modern political democracy.

(6). All previous social systems showed relations inverse to those characterizing capitalism. Value did not dominate society. Economic laws and labor exploitation were transparent. Society was dominated by a power to which the economic logic was subject. The ideology required for reproduction of the system was characterized by metaphysical alienation.

This was my reading of Marx's *Capital* and of Marxism, as can be seen in my doctoral thesis in 1957 and repeated in many of my subsequent works.[1] This reading was not the conventional reading of historical Marxism, still less of its Soviet vulgate. The latter was an economist reduction alienated from historical materialism that quite effaced the specific character of capitalism, reduced the relationship of base-to-superstructure to a single model that was similar for the periods before capitalism to what it was under capitalism. It offered an evolutionist reading of history, sloughing off the progress of the productive forces.

My reading of historical materialism led me to refuse to

treat it as a chapter of the broader philosophy described as dialectical materialism and based on the search for laws common to nature and society. I always rejected this version of historical Marxism (the Soviet diamat). I believed that the laws governing society had an epistemological status qualitatively different from those governing nature. This has always been my position, at least since the late 1950s, and is expressed in my early books. I explained the relationship I saw between diamat and the precapitalist philosophies in a later book and returned to my rejection of diamat in an article.[2]

PRECAPITALIST SOCIAL FORMATIONS AND UNEQUAL DEVELOPMENT

I was won over at once by the *Grundrisse* and the questions Marx raised in it. Understanding of the precapitalist past is not only a desirable scientific pursuit; the interpretation made of it is a vital component in understanding the present and identifying appropriate means to transform it. I already had this belief when I became aware of *Formen*—belatedly—in the mid-1960s.[3] My enthusiasm did not go so far as to accept all of Marx's hypotheses, especially about the Asiatic mode of production. I had already thought about this in terms of the history of the Arab and Islamic East. I had strong reservations about the interpretation, although then it was known only through the simplifications of Karl Wittfogel.[4] I—and doubtless most people—adhered to the conventional thesis of historical Marxism put forward since the Second International and popularized by Stalinism, but I was not satisfied by it. It was a theory of five stages: primitive communism, slavery, feudalism, capitalism, socialism.

I set myself the task of clarifying these issues for myself. I had never had any taste for "Marxology." My concern was not to read between the lines of the *Grundrisse*, but, with Marx's method as inspiration, to integrate into a new interpretation of history all that could be learned since Marx through the reading of scientific studies of precapitalist societies. This gradually led me to the concepts of the communal mode and the ideology of kinship, the tributary mode, and metaphysical dominance exercised by the political power. It led to the concept of systems of tributary societies linked by long-distance trade, cultural spheres defined by the tributary ideology peculiar to each, and central and peripheral forms of the tributary mode defined by the degree of centralization of surplus. It led to the exceptional character of slavery and the connection of slavery to commodity relations and the absence, except in the interstices, of simple commodity production. On the basis of this renewed historical materialism, I reached a major conclusion: the same fundamental contradictions operated in all tributary societies, paving the way for capitalism as an objectively necessary solution to these contradictions. In the more flexible peripheral forms, such as European feudalism, the barriers to the acceleration of the transformation toward capitalism offered less resistance, and this explained the "European miracle."

I began in 1972 to publish these propositions on precapitalist formations, long-distance trade, and the blockage of commercial and tributary formations. I supplemented them in the mid-1970s and considered the matter of cultural spheres and the relations between ideology, science, and technology. I went on to systematize my views on the Arab world.[5] Several of my first formulations remained hazy because ambiguous terminology did not allow the peripheral character of feudalism to be exposed. Some propositions I revised. For the Arab world, for example, I suggested a different equilibrium between the dominant tributary aspect and the role of long-distance trade from that proposed earlier.[6]

I remain satisfied with what I said in 1979 about the assessment of history, the precapitalist formations, and the transition to capitalism. I later added to the argument. I provided a synthesis of my conclusions in 1988. Two recent articles provide an overview.[7]

I suggested a further look at the concept of nation that I felt had never been treated seriously by historical Marxism or bourgeois social thought, which had limited themselves to the highly specific experience of Europe, where formation of the nation was concomitant with that of the capitalist market. I suggested a definition of the nation based on the wider concept of centralization of surplus.[8]

My final positions on these matters differ from those of conventional historical Marxism. They are never situated on grounds of Marxology. I rejected the futile exercise of multiplying infinitely the modes of production. I retained two distinct stages—the communal stage and the tributary stage—and all the supposed modes of production found a place as a variant of one or the other.

In the long transition from the communal to the tributary stage, state and social classes were still embryonic. Manifestations of the organization of social power and the related forms of domination and oppression must be carefully distinguished from manifestations of labor exploitation. This was the basis of my critique of the supposed domestic mode of production of a transhistoric character. The necessary appropriate ideology of kinship, which stresses the solidarities of the extended family, clan, tribe, etc., was the basis of social organization.

The thesis of the tributary mode as the general form of the precapitalist state contradicted the two prevailing Eurocentric visions, of two roads and five stages. All the tributary forms shared essential characteristics: transparent extraction of a prevailing economic surplus through noneconomic means linked to the exercise of power (hence the term "tributary"), the dominance of the political and ideological instance, and the expression of the ideology necessary for the reproduction of this kind of society in the form of a dominant metaphysic.

Tributary societies took on a central or peripheral character according to the degree of maturity of the organization of power by the channel through which tributary surplus was centralized and redistributed within the exploiting ruling class. Thus European (and Japanese) feudalism were peripheral forms characterized by fragmentation of feudal surplus in parallel with fragmentation of power. It evolved toward the advanced, central form of this system with the formation of absolute monarchies in the mercantilist age; this brought it close to the central tributary model. At the time it borrowed from the Chinese model the organization of a statist bureaucracy. In the previous feudal period the church in part fulfilled the role of the almost nonexistent state and ensured the ideological cohesion necessary for reproduction of the system.

The communa mode's internal contradictions found their solution in the passage to the tributary mode, not in the resort to slavery. The latter was always the exception, not the rule, and appeared in close relation to the extension of external or in part internalized commodity relations. Slavery had no place unless one includes integration of the slave society in a regional system organized around fairly intensive commodity relations. Slavery then appeared at various stages of the general evolution in the regional systems largely dominated by the communal mode, in the European tributary system at the stage of transition to capitalism, in Atlantic mercantilism, and in industrial capitalism in the nineteenth-century United States.

There was almost never a simple petty commodity production in a pure or dominant form. Segments of petty commodity production often flourished in the interstices of communal societies or tributary societies especially. This factor drew attention to the networks of societies linked by long-distance trade, an aspect often scorned by the "anticirculationist" prejudice of vulgar Marxism. Tributary societies of the eastern hemisphere formed a system in which a special position was held by three centers—the Islamic, the Chinese, and the Indian—and the peripheries—European, African, Japanese, and Southeast Asian.

The same fundamental contradictions operated in all tributary societies and allowed free rein to expansion of protocapitalist forms and their freedom from subjection to the logic of the tributary power. This conflict could be resolved only in the outcome of capitalism, which implied transformation of the role of the political instance and its cooption by capital. The "European miracle" is explained by the fact that the centralized power of the absolute monarchies came late and was based on an equilibrium between the declining feudalists and the rising bourgeoisie, whereas in the central tributary forms power was entirely and exclusively the preserve of the tributary exploiting class.

If there are for each defined stage appropriate laws governing its reproduction, there are no "laws of transition," merely a dynamism toward ousting the old system and replace it with a new system.

The idea of nation corresponds to a social phenomenon found at various stages of evolution whenever surplus is relatively centralized—through a channel of power for the tributary era nations, through the market for the capitalist nations. In European history, precisely because of the peripheral form of feudalism, the birth of nations was concomitant with the birth of capitalism. In the advanced tributary formations there was sometimes an analogous social phenomenon generated by the centralization of surplus. Historical Marxism focused on the European case and ignored the other phenomenon.

THE CULTURAL ASPECT

I have always insisted on the specific character of capitalism. I have always rejected and criticized an evolutionist analysis.[9] This led me to contrast tributary cultural forms and the culture of capitalism. The tributary forms were necessarily varied, as they were defined by an ideological, often religious, factor. The capitalist forms had a universal application and were defined not by the region where capitalism was born but by the social content of commodity alienation.[10] This consideration led me to the conclusion that the modern world culture is not Western but capitalist.[11]

Capitalism was not capable of fully taking up the universal application it sought. Its development is polarizing at the level of the economic base in which it is deployed. This creates a specific cultural contradiction between the erosion it wreaks on the periphery and the prior cultures and its inability to satisfy the aspirations of those peoples within the framework of capitalism. I noted the erosion of cultural diversity subjected to the conquering hand of Europe.[12] I offered some additional thoughts on the socialist reconstruction necessary for the advent of a truly universal culture.[13]

I also offered a critique of what I have described as culturalist reactions trapping the struggles of the peoples of the periphery in an impasse. By culturalism I mean a claim that different cultures are characterized by transhistoric invariants that determine differing historical trajectories. On this basis I offered a dual critique of European culturalism and outdated Islamic fundamentalism.[14] I reflected on the Islamic case in writings in Arabic from 1985 to 1992, and wrote an article in French on the abortion of the cultural revolution in the Islamic world.[15] I repeated the conclusions of my Arabic writings in a book in French in 1988 when I called on historical Marxism to make a self-criticism of its Eurocentrism.[16] I had already suggested that Marxism should be bolder in its Asian and African vocation.[17]

My thinking about the Islamic world led me back to the tributary ideologies to expose more clearly the role of the dominant metaphysics and the issues it raised.[18] I considered the cosmogony of the search for absolute truth, the methods of reconciling faith and reason, the various forms of expression—by the elite, the masses, and the authorities. I stressed the rupture through which the new capitalist ideology was made manifest, in contrast to the former metaphysical dominance: stress on the search for relative truth, relegation of metaphysical concerns to the realm of private religion, secularism and the modern concept of democracy, the forms in which the revolution was effected within the framework of European Christianity, etc. I have extended these reflections to the central issue of the place of metaphysics in human consciousness.[19]

I was led back to the issue of the formation of the tributary system and suggested dating its birth to Hellenism, and the successive forms it took in Europe and the Middle East shown in the spread of Eastern Christianity, Islam, and Western Christianity. I considered in the same terms the legacies of Confucius, Buddha, and Zarathustra. This led me to reexamine the issue of tributary societies in the Eastern hemisphere from 500 B.C. to 1500 A.D. I drew attention to the pivotal role of the Islamic world of central Asia, as the only region to have benefitted from intensive relations with all the other regions of the ancient world.[20]

I shall end this topic by recalling that in considering Eurocentrism I tried to trace the stages in its construction and its manifestations in the "Christianophile" myth, the myth of Greek ancestry, the artificial construct of "Orientalism," and ineradicable racism.[21]

THE FUTURE OF CAPITALISM AND THE SOCIALIST CHALLENGE

Historical materialism does not look only to the past. It provides the weapons for a critique of the present required to promote its transformation. I also always took seriously Marx's twenty-first Thesis on Feuerbach: "The philosophers have only interpreted the world in various ways; the point is to change it." That is precisely why I have always rejected the analogy of the social sciences and the natural sciences, and the diamat criticized above.

My interpretation of Marxism ruled out any evolutionism to restore to the subjectivity of human action its place in the dialectic of productive forces, productive relations, and social relations. I was therefore critical of the economistic reduction of Soviet vulgar Marxism, from 1960 on at least. My central concern with polarization in the actually existing capitalist world system demanded a vision of the transition beyond capitalism substantially different from that propagated by historical Marxism and I shall retrace the steps in its formulation.

Economism leads to a course of action based on scrupulous regard for the supposedly necessary adaptation to development of the productive forces whose spontaneous expansion seems to take the form of a natural, or supernatural, force replacing the deity. Economic alienation reduces Marxism to a form of bourgeois ideology with which it shares the same basic evolutionist concept. I have returned many times to this critique of Sovietism as the heir to the Marxism of the Second International.[22]

In line with this repeated critique of economism, I observed that the surrender to the supposed laws of natural evolution led not to the supplanting of capitalist relations by socialism but to statism as the product of the increasing centralization of capital. A particular interpretation of class struggle by the labor movement bureaucracy corresponding with the outlook of the technocrats tended to make this likely. The "socialist revolution" against capital would end up benefiting a third party in the new statist class. Elsewhere I suggested an analogy with the anti-feudal peasant revolution playing the game of the third party of the time in the bourgeoisie. I refer here to my observations on the possible convergence of the Western and Soviet systems and the contradictory character of the transition to socialism.[23] These observations are doubtless out of date now that the Soviet statist mode has finally been seen to be a precursor to the restoration of capitalism.

The critique of economism and of its diamat led me to distinguish between evolutionary forms dominated by ideological intervention and conscious political and social action, and those in which objective necessity leads to chaos. I contrasted revolution and decadence.[24]

I shall say no more in this chapter about my criticism of Sovietism, which has been a perpetual topic over the thirty years from 1960 to 1990, or of my reading of Maoism, which I saw as a counter to Soviet economism.[25]

The dual analysis constantly raised basic questions about the goal of communism, its relation to a socialist utopia, the role of the market as an expression of economistic aliena-tion and how to prevent that. Would it be prevented artificially by bureaucratic decision or incorporated into democratic and nonalienated progressive social planning? Was the state going to wither away? Would it be trans-formed into an administration of things and not a govern-ment of human beings? It raised the issue of nation and of cultural diversity.

In the dual analysis I tried to link the convergent or divergent changes in the USSR and China to their internal social dynamic in one respect and to the modalities of their incorporation into the world system in another. I refer to Chapter 7 and the interpretation of East-West conflict within the global hegemonic plan of the United States. I refer to earlier writings on the USSR and China.[26] In a word, the post-Maoist option of China's state and Communist Party leadership was an attempt to hasten the opening to capitalist development while maintaining state and party control over the process. This seemed to me dangerous and ineffective. The alternative was to strengthen democracy through control by the people over the concessions to be made to capitalism.

In all these analyzes I remained caught in the old paradigm of the "transition to socialism," a term I retained until jettisoning it in the mid-1980s. Through my critique of the strategies of socialist construction I perceived an alternative of a different character, and after 1992 I described it as national and popular. This was the logical consequence of my central position on capitalist polarization.

The critique in Chapter 6 of the development experiences in the third world led me to the conclusion that the strategies of overt integration into the world system were bound to reproduce and widen polarization, and that the strategies of the radical wing of the national liberation movement were, despite appearances, no different.

I criticized the Soviet talk of the so-called noncapitalist road.[27] I preferred a realistic analysis of the world political system, like that China's three worlds thesis, which seemed to me to have been valid, at least at the point when it was enunciated.

More generally, analysis of the consequences of polarization always brought me back to the issue of the nation as a subject of history. Was it only a screen for social classes, as I had once asked?[28] I returned here to the national question in the centers. I criticized the concepts of Marx who preferred the bourgeoisie to the peasants, precisely because he underestimated the real effects of capitalist polarization. On the issue of the nation as subject of history I noted the remarkable correlation in European history of the bourgeois state, an autocentric capitalist national productive system, and the nation. I noted its failure elsewhere and the harmful effect of the transfer of the ideology of nation in these circumstances.[29]

In Chapter 6 I drew conclusions from my own critique of development. I do not believe that delinking is utopian, as it has been described in the mostly superficial critiques made of it, but rather the only realistic response to the liberal utopia. I would also recall that the alternative of delinking does not exclude parallel action to influence the world system and make it adjust to the demands of delinking.

The more I sharpened my critique of development, the more I realized it applied just as much to the countries of the East and called into question the old paradigm of the transition to socialism established by the Second International and inherited by Bolshevism. I noted in this respect that the "hundred-year revolution" for socialism implied sharp breaks on the periphery and a long positional war in the center to be conducted at the same time. I recently addressed the implications of this new approach for postcapitalism for the peripheries, and on the scale of the world system as a whole.[30]

I analyze the period from 1945 to 1990 as resting on three pillars: Western capitalist Fordism, Sovietism in the Eastern countries, and developmentalism in the third world or bourgeois national liberation in the South. They have now collapsed and brought ideological and organizational crises to all parts of the world. I reread the history of the interrupted anti-imperialist revolutions in Mexico, Turkey, and Egypt, of the uninterrupted Chinese revolution and the transition to socialism. I question the old paradigms of national liberation. I suggest a new paradigm based on a national and popular alliance, the element of democracy, and the role of the intelligentsia.

I also believe it necessary to situate the new strategic issues in the framework of a geopolitical analysis that takes account of the end of the cycle of Sovietism and the new U.S. military hegemony.[31] In conclusion, I recall the final pages of *Empire of Chaos* and the three stages in the struggle for socialism: Socialism I, from 1880 to 1914; Socialism II, from 1917 to 1990; and Socialism III, still to be built.

Notes

1. THE POSTWAR PERIOD, 1945-1992: AN OVERVIEW

1. See my articles "À propos de la régulation," published in Arabic in *The Arab Economic Review*, no. 1 (1992): 7-24; "Trente ans de critique du système sovietique 1960-1990," *Africa Development* 16, no. 2 (1991): 73-94, and partially in English in "Thirty Years of Critique of the Soviet System," *Monthly Review* 44, no. 1 (1992): 43-50; and "Il y a trente ans, Bandoung" published in 1985 and collected in the revised and expanded edition of *L'Échange inégal et la loi de la valeur* (Paris: Economica, 1988; hereafter *L'Échange inégal*).

2. ESTABLISHING THE GLOBAL ECONOMIC SYSTEM, 1945-1955

1. From November 1949 to February 1953, sixteen issues of the journal *Étudiants Anticolonialistes* appeared under the direction of Jacques Vergès. Contributors included officials of the Association des Étudiants Musulmans Nord-africains (AEMNA), the Vietnamese Vo The Quang and Do Dai Phuoc, students from Reunion and the Caribbean (Justin, Fardin), and my first sub-Saharan African friends (Malik Sangaret, Abdou Moumouni). The journal supported peace for Vietnam, for North Korea, and for Egypt during partisan attacks on the Suez Canal in 1951.
2. I recall the African personalities Gabriel d'Arboussier, Félix

Houphouët Boigny, Félix Tchicaya, Ouezzin Coulibaly, Mamadou Konaté, Doudou Guèye, Léopold Sedar Senghor, Ahmed Sékou Touré, Keita Fodeba, Alioune Diop, Ruben Um Nyobé, and the Caribbeans Aimé Césaire and Léon Damas.

3. From June 1949 to July 1953, twenty-five issues of the journal *Moyen Orient* appeared under the direction of Maxime Rodinson. Contributors included Ismail Abdallah; Iraj Eskandari, a Tudeh Party leader; Raymond Aghion; and Yves Bénot. It produced interesting studies such as a history of Tudeh and of the Muslim Brotherhood. It advocated the notion of Arab neutralism several years ahead of the Bandung era.

4. "Les Effets structurels de l'intégration internationale des économies précapitalistes: Une Étude théorique du mécanisme qui a engendré les économies dites sous-développées" [The structural effects of the international integration of precapitalist economies: A theoretical study of the mechanism that has engendered the so-called underdeveloped economies] (Paris: University of Paris, 1957, hereafter "Les Effets structurels").

5. See Samir Amin, *L'Accumulation à l'échelle mondiale* (Paris: Anthropos, 1970), and in English, *Accumulation on a World Scale*, 2 vols. (New York: Monthly Review Press, 1974, hereafter *Accumulation*).

3. THE THEORY OF CAPITAL ACCUMULATION: ITS FORMATION AND EVOLUTION

1. See *Accumulation*.

2. Paul Baran and Paul Sweezy, *Monopoly Capital* (New York: Monthly Review Press, 1966), especially pp. 8-10.

3. Arghiri Emmanuel, *Unequal Exchange: A Study of the Imperialism of Trade* (New York: Monthly Review Press, 1969).

4. Samir Amin, "The End of a Debate," *Imperialism and Unequal Development* (New York: Monthly Review Press, 1977), p. 438. This first appeared as the Afterword in the second edition of *L'Accumulation à l'échelle mondiale* (Paris: Anthropos, 1971).

5. The latter two are available in English as *Imperialism and Unequal Development* and *The Law of Value and Historical Materialism* (New York: Monthly Review Press, 1978).
6. See also "Can Environmental Problems Be Subject to Economic Calculations?" *World Development* 20 (April 1992): 523-30.
7. Samir Amin, *The Arab Economy Today* (London: Zed, 1982). Note especially Chapter 5, "The Use of Arab Labour Power."
8. Samir Amin, *Class and Nation, Historically and in the Current Crisis* (New York: Monthly Review Press, 1980).
9. See "L'exploitation des paysans du tiers monde," published in 1981 and included in *L'Échange inégal;* see also Samir Amin, *La Déconnexion: Pour sortir du système mondial* (Paris: Découverte, 1985); this is available in English as *Delinking: Towards a Polycentric World* (London: Zed, 1990, hereafter *Delinking*).
10. See "Une Stratégie de développement autocentrée est-elle possible pour l'Afrique?" published in 1982 and collected in *L'échange inégal;* see also Samir Amin, "Is an Endogenous Development Strategy Possible in Africa?" in Krishna Ahooja-Patel et al., eds., *World Economy in Transition* (Oxford: Pergamon, 1986).
11. Samir Amin et al., *Transforming the Revolution: Social Movements and the World-System* (New York: Monthly Review Press, 1990, hereafter *Transforming the Revolution*).
12. Samir Amin, "Income Distribution in the Capitalist System," *Review* 8, no. 1 (1984): 328.
13. Samir Amin, *L'Avenir du Maoïsme* (Paris: Minuit, 1981); available in English as *The Future of Maoism* (New York: Monthly Review Press, 1981).

4. THE GLOBALIZATION OF CAPITAL: CENTER-PERIPHERY POLARIZATION

1. See my articles "The Ancient World-Systems versus the Modern Capitalist World-System," *Review* 14, no. 3 (1991): 349-85; "Capitalisme et système monde," *Sociologie et Sociétes* (1992).
2. See *Transforming the Revolution,* pp. 103-09.

3. See *Accumulation* and *Le Développement inégal* (Paris: Minuit, 1973), available in English as *Unequal Development* (New York: Monthly Review Press, 1976).
4. Paul Sweezy et al., *The Transition from Feudalism to Capitalism* (London: New Left Books, 1976).
5. See *Unequal Development; Class and Nation.*
6. See "La Formation du système mondial," first published in 1975 and collected in *Impérialisme et sous-développement en Afrique,* 2nd ed. (Paris: Economica, 1988); "On European Development and the Third World" (1988); J. M. Blaut, "Colonialism and the Rise of Capitalism," *Science and Society* 53, no. 3 (1989): 260–96; Samir Amin, "Colonialism and the Rise of Capitalism: A Comment [on J.M. Blaut]," *Science and Society* 54, no. 2 (1990): 67–72; Samir Amin, "1492," *Monthly Review* 44, no. 3 (1992): 10–19.
7. See "The Ancient World-Systems versus the Modern Capitalist World-System" and "Capitalisme et système monde."
8. See *Unequal Development,* pp. 22, 59–72.
9. See *Imperialism and Unequal Development,* pp. 103–16.
10. See Samir Amin "Crisis, Nationalism, and Socialism" in Samir Amin et al., *Dynamics of Global Crisis* (New York: Monthly Review Press, and London, Macmillan, 1982), pp. 167–231; Samir Amin et al., *La Crise de l'impérialisme* (Paris: Minuit, 1975)
11. See *Unequal Development* and "Capitalisme et système monde."
12. See Samir Amin, *Empire of Chaos* (New York: Monthly Review Press, 1992).
13. See "Capitalisme et système monde."
14. See *Unequal Development;* "La Formation du système mondial"; and "La Lutte pour le contrôle du système mondial" (1982) in *Impérialisme et sous-développement en Afrique;* see also "The Struggle for Control of the World Capitalist Order," *Monthly Review,* 34, no. 1 (1982): 47–53.
15. See "Capitalisme et système monde."
16. See an overview in my "La régulation" (1992).
17. See "Accumulation and Development: A Theoretical Model," *Review of African Political Economy* 1 (1974): 9–26.
18. Compare "America Latina en la economía mundial," seminar in tribute to Dr. Raul Prebisch (Santiago de Chile: UN/ECLA, 1988).
19. See *Imperialism and Unequal Development,* pp. 232–33.
20. See *Unequal Development,* pp. 298-317, 317-33; Samir Amin

under the pseudonym Hassan Riad, *L'Égypte nasserienne* (Paris: Minuit, 1964); Samir Amin, *The Maghreb in the Modern World* (Harmondsworth: Penguin, 1970); Samir Amin, *Trois Expériences africaines de développement: Le Mali, La Guinée et le Ghana* (Paris: Presses Universitaires de France, 1965); *Le Développement du capitalisme en Côte d'Ivoire* (Paris: Minuit, 1967); *Le Monde des affaires sénégalais* (Paris: Minuit, 1969); *Neo-Colonialism in West Africa* (Harmondsworth: Penguin, 1973); and Samir Amin and Catherine Coquery-Vidrovitch, *Histoire économique du Congo 1880-1968* (Paris: Anthropos, 1969).

21. See my essay first published anonymously as "The Class Struggle in Africa," *Révolution Africa Latin America Asia* 9 (1964): 23-47; "Le Développement du capitalisme en Afrique noire" (1969), *L'Homme et la Société* 6 (1967): 107-19 and "Sous-développement et dépendance en Afrique noire" (1972), both collected in *Impérialisme et sous-développement en Afrique;* see also "Underdevelopment and Dependence in Black Africa—Origins and Contemporary Forms," *Journal of Modern African Studies* 10, no. 4 (1972): 503-24.

22. See Samir Amin, *The Arab Nation* (London: Zed, 1978) and my article "État, politique et économie dans le monde arabe," mimeographed, CIDMAA, Montreal; published in Arabic in *Al Moustaqbal al Arabi* (Beyrouth), no. 164 (October 1992): 4-26.

23. See "Sous-développement et dépendance en Afrique noire" (1972) and "Le développement du capitalisme en Afrique noire," both collected in *L'Échange inégal et la loi de la valeur,* expanded edition (Paris: Economica, 1988).

24. See "À propos du NOEI, et de l'avenir des relations économiques internationales," *Africa Development* 4 (1978), included in *Impérialisme et sous-développement en Afrique;* "The role of trade and industry in development," presented in Vienna in 1989 at the conference "Ten Years After the Brandt Report," also collected in *Impérialisme et sous-développement en Afrique.*

25. See *La Crise de l'impérialisme; Imperialism and Unequal Development,* pp. 103-16; *The Law of Value and Historical Materialism,* pp. 76-77.

26. See *Imperialism and Unequal Development,* p. 115.

27. See *La Crise de l'impérialisme,* pp. 19 ff.

28. See "Capitalism, State Collectivism, and Socialism," *Monthly Review* 29, no. 2 (1977): 25-41.
29. See "Il y a trente ans, Bandoung" and my return to the subject in *Delinking*, pp. 15-17.
30. See my foreword to Azzam Mahjoub, ed., *Adjustment or Delinking? The African Experience* (Tokyo: United Nations University and London: Zed, 1990).
31. See the joint introduction to *Transforming the Revolution* and its reference to the earlier *Dynamics of Global Crisis*.
32. See "The End of a Debate."
33. See *La Crise de l'impérialisme*, pp. 19 ff.
34. See *Delinking*, p. 14.
35. See *Transforming the Revolution*.
36. See *La Crise de l'impérialisme*, p. 33.
37. See "L'Impérialisme" (1976) in *L'Échange inégal*, pp. 137-38; and "Capitalism, State Collectivism, and Socialism," pp. 39-40.
38. See *Class and Nation*, pp. 139-41.
39. See forewords in Faysal Yachir, *Mining in Africa Today* (Tokyo: United Nations University and London: Zed, 1988); Smail Khenass, *Le Defi énergétique en Méditerranée* (Paris: Harmattan, 1992); Faysal Yachir, *La Méditerranée dans la révolution technologique* (Paris: Harmattan, 1992); Hamid Ait Amara and Bernard Founou-Tchuigoua, eds., *African Agriculture: The Critical Choices* (Tokyo: United Nations University and London: Zed, 1990); Hamid Ait Amara, *L'Agriculture mediterranenne dans les rapports Nord-Sud* (Paris: Harmattan, 1992); Charbel Zarour, *La Coopération arabo-africaine* (Paris: Harmattan, 1989).
40. See *Dynamics of Global Crisis*, p. 187.
41. See *Dynamics of Global Crisis*, p. 195.
42. See *Dynamics of Global Crisis*, p. 208.
43. See *Dynamics of Global Crisis*, pp. 188-89.
44. See "The End of a Debate" and "L'exploitation des paysans du tiers monde."
45. See "La Crise, le tiers-monde, les relations Nord-Sud, Est-Ouest" (1983), collected in *L'Échange inégal*; *Delinking* "Une autre configuration des relations internationales Ouest-Est-Sud est-elle souhaitable, probable, possible?" in Sofia Mappa, ed., *La CEE: chance ou contrainte pour la transformation sociale* (Paris: Harmattan, 1989).

46. See *Delinking* p. 24.
47. See *Delinking* pp. 37-40, 97-99.
48. See *Empire of Chaos.*
49. See Samir Amin, *Les Enjeux stratégiques en Méditerranée* (Paris: Harmattan, 1992), p. 34.

5. THE BOURGEOIS NATIONAL PROJECT IN THE THIRD WORLD, 1955-1990

1. See *The Future of Maoism.*
2. See *L'Égypte nasserienne.*
3. See *The Maghreb in the Modern World.*
4. See *Trois Expériences africaines de développement.*
5. See translator's note in Amilcar Cabral, *Unity and Struggle* (New York: Monthly Review Press, 1979, and London, Heinemann, 1980), p. 136.
6. From September 1963 to December 1964, thirteen issues of the journal *Révolution* appeared (with an English edition published in London, first as *African Revolution* then as *Revolution Africa Latin America Asia*) under the direction of Jacques Vergès. The editorial board included Abdul Rahman Mohamed Babu (Zanzibar), Viriato da Cruz (Angola), Mamadou Gologo (Mali), Samba Ndiaye (Senegal), Rabah Bitat (Algeria), Carlos Franqui (Cuba), Cheddi Jagan (Guyana), Martin Legassick (South Africa), Hamza Alavi (Pakistan), Nguyen Kien (Vietnam), Hassan Riad [i.e. Samir Amin] (Egypt). It was an early starter in the critical analysis of Sovietism.
7. The IDEP team allowed the establishment of the first networks for Africa-wide debate with Kwame Ninsin, Emmanuel Hansen, Josephine Guissou, Brito, Kwesi Jonah, Fui S. Tsikata, Carlos Lopes, Harris Memel-Fotê, Mahamadou Maiga, Denis Traore, Michel Keita, Talata Kafando, Okwudiba Nnoli, Ikenna Nzimiro, Claude Ake, Akin Fadahunsi, Marie-Angelique Savane, Amady Aly Deng (West Africa); Kankwenda M'baya, Georges Nzongola-Ntalaja, Mario de Andrade, Henri Lopes. Pierre Mousssa, Jacques Depelchin (Central Africa); Issa Shivji, Mahmood Mamdani, Taye Gurmu, Abdalla Bujra, Dharam Ghai,

Darga, Mohamed Aden, Haroub Othman, Dan Nabudere (East Africa); Ibbo Mandaza, Nathan Shamuyarira, Manandafy, Derrick Chitala, Gilbert Mudenda (Southern Africa); Fawzi Mansour, Faysal Yachir, Hamid Ait Amara, Smail Khenass, Mohamed Ali Tayseer, Azzam Mahjoub, Ali El-Kenz, Abdallah Saaf, Thami El-Khyari, Fredj Stambouli (North Africa). From these teams emerged the founding group of the Council for the Development of Economic and Social Research in Africa (CODESRIA) and of the Third World Forum constituted at Santiago de Chile in April 1973. IDEP and the Third World Forum have developed a common line of action with our Latin American colleagues that brings in the main figures of the "dependency school": Celso Furtado, Fernando Henrique Cardoso, Ruy Mauro Marini, Theotonio Dos Santos, Darcy Ribeiro, Pablo Gonzalez Casanova, Enrique Oteiza, Pedro Vuskovic, Andre Gunder Frank, Gerard Pierre-Charles, Norman Girvan, Hector Silva Michelena, Xabier Gorostiaga, Anibal Quijano. Working relations were also established with our colleagues from Asia: Amiya Kumar Bagchi, Bipan Chandra, Ramkrishna Mukherjee, Paresh Chattopadhyay, S. Husin Ali, Jomo Kwame Sundaram, Eqbal Ahmad, Renato Constantino, George Aseniero, Suthy Prasartset. During the 1970s the battle of the Group of 77 within the UN was at its height. Founders of the Third World Forum included national and international personalities waging the battle, such as Enrique Iglesias, Gamani Corea, Nurul Islam, Alister McIntyre, Justinian Rweyemamu, Enrique Oteiza, Yousif Sayegh, and Ismail-Sabri Abdallah (elected chairman of the Third World Forum after the Karachi congress in 1975), and many others.

6. CRITICAL ANALYSIS OF DEVELOPMENT THEORY, 1955-1990

1. See Aidan Foster, "The Empirical Samir Amin: A Notice and Appreciation," the introduction to *The Arab Economy Today.*
2. See *L'Égypte nasserienne.*
3. See *Unequal Development* and *The Arab Nation.*

4. See "Les Contradictions du développement capitaliste en Égypte" (1984) collected in *Impérialisme et sous-développement en Afrique;* see also "Contradictions in the Capital Development of Egypt," *Monthly Review* 36, no. 4 (1984): 13-21; and "État, économie et politique dans le monde arabe" (1992).

5. See Samir Amin, *L'Économie du Maghreb,* 2 vols. (Paris: Minuit, 1966); *The Maghreb in the Modern World; Irak et Syrie: 1960-1980* (Paris: Minuit, 1982); *The Arab Economy Today.*

6. See *The Maghreb in the Modern World,* pp. 239-42.

7. See five main books: *Trois expériences africaines de développement; Le développement du capitalisme en Côte d'Ivoire; Le Monde des affaires sénégalais; Neo-Colonialism in West Africa;* and *Histoire économique du Congo 1880-1968.* See also "Le développement du bassin du fleuve Sénégal" (1972) and "La Republique de Guinée" (1972), both collected in *Impérialisme et sous-développement en Afrique.* See further my introduction to Samir Amin, ed., *Modern Migrations in Western Africa* (Oxford: Oxford University Press, 1974).

8. This distinction is made in *Neo-Colonialism in West Africa, Histoire économique du Congo 1880-1968,* and "Underdevelopment and Dependence in Black Africa."

9. See Samir Amin, "Transitional Phases in Sub-Saharan Africa: A Review," *Monthly Review* 25, no. 5 (1973): 52-57.

10. See *Le Monde des affaires sénégalais.*

11. See *Modern Migrations in Western Africa,* pp. 81, 102.

12. See my review of Mario Pinto de Andrade and Marc Ollivier, *La Guerre en Angola* (Paris: Maspero, 1971), "L'Afrique du Sud" (1971), and "Les perspectives de l'Afrique australe" (1977), all collected in *Impérialisme et sous-développement en Afrique;* and "The Future of Southern Africa," *Journal of Southern African Affairs* 2, no. 3 (1977); and Samir Amin, Derrick Chitala, and Ibbo Mandaza, eds., *SADCC: Prospects for Disengagement and Development in Southern Africa* (Tokyo: United Nations University and London: Zed, 1987).

13. See various analyses by Pierre Beaudet.

14. See "Les limites de la révolution verte" (1970), "Développement et transformations structurelles en Afrique" (1973), "L'industrialisation au service de l'agriculture" (1981), and "Critique du rapport de la Banque Mondiale pour l'Afrique," in

Impérialisme et sous-développement en Afrique. See also "A Critique of the World Bank Report Entitled 'Accelerated Development in Sub-Saharan Africa,'" *Africa Development* 7, nos. 1-2 (1982): 23–29. See also "Une strategie de développement autocentree est-elle possible pour l'Afrique?" in *L'Échange inégal.* See further, "The interlinkage between agricultural revolution and industrialization" (1988); "The role of trade and industry in development" (1989); foreword to Thami El-Khyari, *Agriculture au Maroc* (Casablanca: Editions OKAD, 1987); foreword to Mohamed Lamine Gakou, *The Crisis in African Agriculture* (London: Zed, 1990); foreword to Hamid Ait Amara, *L'Agriculture méditerranéenne dans les rapports Nord-Sud* (Paris: Harmattan, 1992).

15. See forewords in Faysal Yachir, *Mining in Africa Today,* Smail Khenass, *Le Defi énergétique en Méditerranée,* and Faysal Yachir, *La Méditerranée dans la révolution technologique.*

16. See Samir Amin, "Underpopulated Africa," collected in *Impérialisme et sous-développement en Afrique.*

17. See introduction to "Problemes actuels de l'unité africaine" (Algiers: SNED, 1972), collected in *Impérialisme et sous-développement en Afrique.*

18. See forewords in Charbel Zarour, *La Coopération arabo-africaine* and Charbel Zarour, *La Coopération arabo-sénégalaise* (Paris: Harmattan, 1989).

19. See "Pour un aménagement du système monétaire des pays africains de la zone franc" (1969) and "Zone franc et développement" (1972), both collected in *Impérialisme et sous-développement en Afrique.*

20. See *The Arab Nation,* pp. 7–8.

21. See Samir Amin, *Eurocentrism* (New York, Monthly Review Press, 1989), and my writings in Arabic from 1985 to 1990.

22. See "État, politique et économie dans le monde arabe" (1992).

23. See foreword in Yildiz Sertel, *Nord-Sud: Crise et immigration: le cas turc* (Paris: Publisud, 1987).

24. See *The Arab Nation;* and Samir Amin, "Conditions for Autonomy in the Mediterranean Region" in Faysal Yachir, *The Mediterranean: Between Autonomy and Dependency* (Tokyo: United Nations University and London: Zed, 1989).

25. See "Le Conflit du Moyen Orient dans une Perspective Mondiale" in Bichara Khader, ed., *La Coopération Euro-Arabe,* vol.

3 (Louvain, Belgium: University of Louvain, 1982); and *Les Enjeux stratégiques.*

26. See "The Class Struggle in Africa"; "Le développement du capitalisme en Afrique noire"; "Underdevelopment and Dependence in Black Africa—Origins and Contemporary Forms"; and "Transitional Phases in Sub-Saharan Africa."

27. See *Class and Nation,* pp. 176-77.

28. See "L'État et le développement," *Socialism in the World,* 58 (1987): 29-49; and "La Question democratique dans le Tiers-monde contemporain," *Africa Development* 14, no. 2 (1989): 5-25 and "The Issue of Democracy in the Contemporary Third World," *Socialism and Democracy* 12 (1991): 83-104.

29. See foreword in Michel Capron, ed., *L'Europe face au Sud, les relations avec le monde arabe et africain* (Paris: Harmattan, 1991).

30. See "Peace, National and Regional Security and Development: Some Reflections on the African Experience," *Alternatives* 14, no. 2 (1989): 215-29.

31. See my articles: "UNCTAD III, A Critical Appraisal," 1973; "UNCTAD IV and the New International Economic Order," *Africa Development* 1, no. 1 (1976): 5-27; "Self-Reliance and the New International Economic Order," *Monthly Review* 29, no. 3 (1977): 1-21; "À propos du NOEI et de l'avenir des relations économiques internationales" (1978), all collected in *Impérialisme et Sous-Développement en Afrique.*

32. See Samir Amin, *La Faillité du développement en Afrique et dans le Tiers Monde* (Paris: Harmattan, 1989) and in English, Samir Amin, *Maldevelopment: Anatomy of a Global Failure* (Tokyo: United Nations University and London, Zed, 1990); "À propos du rapport de la commission Brandt" (1980); "Il y a trente ans, Bandoung"; "Nationalisme," in *Palgrave Dictionary of Economics* (London: Macmillan, 1989); foreword to *Adjustment or Delinking? The African Experience.*

33. See *Delinking* and *Maldevelopment.*

34. See *Delinking,* pp. 63-66; "Le tiers-monde et la révolution," *Sociologica Ruralis* 22, no. 1 (1990): 93; "La Déconnexion incontournable" (1992).

35. See "On European Development and the Third World" and "The European experience and the Third World," *Review* 11, no. 1 (1988): 55-66.

36. See foreword to *Adjustment or Delinking? The African Experience.*

37. See "La Déconnexion, la révolution nationale populaire et l'intelligentsia" (1988); "Democracy and National Strategy in the Periphery," *Third World Quarterly* 9, no. 4 (1987): 1129-56; *Transforming the Revolution; Maldevelopment;* and *Empire of Chaos.*

38. See "Les conditions d'une sortie à gauche de la crise" (1983) in *L'Échange inégal;* "Le contexte économique et politique des relations euro-arabes" (1984) in *Impérialisme et sous-développement en Afrique;* "In Favor of a Polycentric World," *IFDA Dossier* 69 (1989): 51-54; *Development/Développement/Desarrollo* 1 (1991), p. 83; "La Maison Commune Europe," *IFDA Dossier* 73 (1989): 41-44; and foreword in Michel Capron, ed., *L'Europe face au Sud, les relations avec le monde arabe et africain.*

39. See *Empire of Chaos* and *Les Enjeux stratégiques.*

7. THE SYSTEM IN CRISIS: A CRITIQUE OF SOVIETISM, 1960-1990

1. See Victor Louis, *The Coming Decline of the Chinese Empire* (New York: Times Books, 1979).

2. See *Empire of Chaos.*

3. See *Empire of Chaos* and "La stratégie politique et militaire d'hégémonie des États-Unis" in *Les Enjeux stratégiques,* pp. 19-53.

8. THE SYSTEM IN CRISIS: THE COLLAPSE OF CAPITALIST REGULATORY MECHANISMS

1. For an overview of the regulation approach see Robert Boyer, *La Théorie de la régulation* (Paris: Decouverte, 1986).

2. See "Capitalisme et système monde."

3. My first formulation of the issue dates to my doctoral thesis published in *Accumulation* and is expressed as a model in "Accumulation and Development: A Theoretical Model"; see also new introduction to the revised *L'Échange inégal.*

4. See "Capitalisme et système monde" (and Chapter 4 of this book).

5. See "Income Distribution in the Capitalist System."

6. This also dates back to my doctoral thesis; see also *Accumulation,* pp. 395–484.

7. See my doctoral thesis and *Accumulation,* pp. 485–534.

8. See my doctoral thesis and *Accumulation,* pp. 535–87.

9. See "Capitalisme et système monde," with a critique of Robert Keohane, "The Theory of Hegemonic Stability" in Ole Holsti et al., *Changes in the International System* (Boulder: Westview Press, 1980).

10. See Ramkrishna Mukherjee, *The Rise and Fall of the East India Company* (New York: Monthly Review Press, 1974), and Amiya Kumar Bagchi's contribution to Samir Amin, ed., *Mondialization et accumulation: Le monde vu du sud* (Paris: Harmattan, 1993).

11. See Harry Braverman, *Labor and Monopoly Capital: The Degradation of Work in the Twentieth Century* (New York, Monthly Review Press, 1974).

12. See *Monopoly Capital;* Paul Sweezy, *The Theory of Capitalist Development* (New York: Monthly Review Press, 1942); Paul Baran, *The Political Economy of Growth* (New York: Monthly Review Press, 1957 and Harmondsworth: Penguin, 1973); Paul Baran, *The Longer View* (New York: Monthly Review Press, 1969); Paul Sweezy, *Modern Capitalism* (New York: Monthly Review Press, 1972); John Bellamy Foster and Henryk Szlajfer, eds., *The Faltering Economy* (New York: Monthly Review Press, 1984); and John Bellamy Foster, *The Theory of Monopoly Capitalism* (New York: Monthly Review Press, 1986).

13. See *Transforming the Revolution* and "Capitalisme et système monde."

14. See *Empire of Chaos, Les Enjeux stratégiques,* especially pp. 19–53; and Samir Amin, "U.S. Militarism in the New World Order," *Social Justice* 19, no. 1 (1992): 1.

15. See Paul Sweezy and Harry Magdoff, "Production and Finance," *Monthly Review* 35, no. 1 (1983): 1–13.

16. See Paul Boccara, "Théories de la régulation et suraccumulation—dévaluation du capital," *Issue* 32 (1988).
17. See Michel Beaud, *L'Économie mondiale dans les années quatre-vingt* (Paris: Decouverte, 1989).
18. See *Empire of Chaos*.
19. See "Capitalisme et système monde."

A NOTE ON HISTORICAL MATERIALISM

1. See *Accumulation; Unequal Development*, pp. 13–58; "The End of a Debate"; The Law of Value and Historical Materialism, pp. 1-7; *Imperialism and Unequal Development*, pp. 1–15, 153–67; *Class and Nation*, pp. 1-15; *Eurocentrism*; "The Ancient World-Systems versus the Modern World-System"; and "Capitalisme et système monde."
2. See *Eurocentrism*, pp. 30–31; and "Historical and Ethical Materialism," *Monthly Review* 45, no. 1 (1993): 44–56.
3. Karl Marx's *Grundrisse* of 1857-1858 was published in two limited-edition German volumes by the Foreign Language Publishers (Moscow, 1939 and 1941) and in a one-volume offset reprint by Dietz Verlag (Berlin, 1953); see extracts in English in Eric Hobsbawm, ed., *Precapitalist Economic Formations* (London: Lawrence and Wishart, 1964). [Translator's note].
4. See Karl Wittfogel, *Oriental Despotism: A Comparative Study of Total Power* (New Haven: Yale University Press, 1957).
5. See *Unequal Development*, pp. 13–22, 30–31, and 66-58; "La Formation du système mondial" (1975); "L'Esclavage en Afrique" (1975) collected in *Impérialisme et sous-développement en Afrique; Imperialism and Unequal Development*, pp. 89-102, 153–67; and *The Arab Nation*.
6. See *The Arab Nation* and *Unequal Development*.
7. See *Class and Nation*, pp. 1-20, 36-70, and 71-103; "La Lutte pour le contrôle du système mondial" (1982), "Esclavage et histoire" (1984), and "Modes de production, histoire et développement inégal" (1985), in *Impérialisme et sous-développement en Afrique*; "The Struggle for Control of the World Capitalist Order; *Eurocentrism*, pp. 71–88; "The Ancient World-Systems versus

the Modern World-System"; and "Capitalisme et système monde."

8. See *Unequal Development*, pp. 27-28, and *Class and Nation*, pp. 9-20.
9. See "The Ancient World-Systems versus the Modern World-System."
10. See *Imperialism and Unequal Development*, pp. 89-102.
11. See *Eurocentrism*, pp. 89-117.
12. See "1492."
13. See *Eurocentrism*, pp. 137-52.
14. See *Delinking* pp. 165-73, 174-88.
15. See "La Fin de la Nahda," *Revue d'Études Palestiniennes* 19 (1986): 81-100.
16. See *Eurocentrism*, pp. 118-23.
17. See *Delinking* pp. 123-64.
18. See *Eurocentrism*, pp. 15-59.
19. See "Historical and Ethical Materialism."
20. See "The Ancient World-Systems versus the Modern World-System."
21. See *Eurocentrism*, pp. 71-78, especially p. 77.
22. See "The End of a Debate"; "Capitalism, State Collectivism, and Socialism," pp. 39-40; *Imperialism and Unequal Development*, pp. 1-8.
23. See *Class and Nation*, p. 207-11.
24. See *La Crise de l'impérialisme* and conclusion to *Class and Nation*, pp. 249-56.
25. See *The Future of Maoism*.
26. See *Delinking* pp. 92-99, and *The Future of Maoism*.
27. See *Class and Nation* and *Dynamics of Global Crisis*.
28. See *Class and Nation*.
29. See *Delinking* pp. 41-84.
30. See "Capitalism, State Collectivism, and Socialism," p. 39; *Transforming the Revolution;* and *Empire of Chaos*.
31. See *Les Enjeux stratégiques*.

Index